SEW NEWS
TIMESAVING
TIPS

from **sew**news magazine

Sew News Timesaving Tips

from the "Sewing With Nancy" series
©1996 by Oxmoor House, Inc.
Book Division of Southern Progress Corporation
PO Box 2463, Birmingham, Alabama 35201

Published by Oxmoor House, Inc., and Leisure Arts, Inc.

Library of Congress Catalog Number: 96-68138
Hardcover ISBN: 0-8487-1467-9
Softcover ISBN: 0-8487-1489-X
Manufactured in the United States of America
First Printing 1996

Editor-in-Chief Nancy Fitzpatrick Wyatt
Senior Crafts Editor Susan Ramey Cleveland
Senior Editor, Editorial Services Olivia Kindig Wells
Art Director James Boone

Sew News Timesaving Tips

Editor Linda Baltzell Wright
Editorial Assistant Wendy Wolford Noah
Copy Editor Katharine R. Wiencke
Designer Clare T. Minges
Production and Distribution Director Phillip Lee
Associate Production Manager Theresa L. Beste
Production Coordinator Marianne Jordan Wilson
Production Assistant Valerie Heard
Senior Photographer John O'Hagan
Photographers Gary Clark, Keith Harrelson, Kevin May Corp.
Photo Stylist Katie Stoddard
Illustrator Chris Hansen

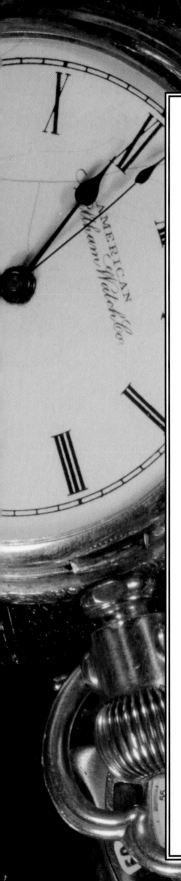

DEDICATED

to all the loyal and supportive *Sew News* readers who inspire us to strive continually for sewing publishing excellence.

THANK YOU!

SPECIAL THANKS

to the *Sew News* **editorial staff members** for their encouraging words and diligent work on the magazine, making the creation of this book possible.

Janet Klaer, *Sew News* contributing editor, our "notions guru," for compiling the "Great Notions" chapter; **Jenny Inserro** for writing assistance.

the *Sew News* **writers** who share their expertise with readers each month.

Keith Griepentrog, often known as "Mr. Sew News," for his unending support *and* computer expertise.

CONTENTS

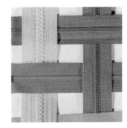

FAST FUSIBLES......67

QUICK CLOSURES 93

MACHINE MAGIC 77

TAKE CARE 105

FOREWORD

Sew News magazine has been *the* sewing publication for well over a decade. At our office, we receive many copies of the magazine, but one "preview" copy arrives several days before the others. Everyone practically scrambles to get first reading privileges. The lucky first reader dog-ears pages or sticks on yellow Post-it notes to mark articles of inspiration and sewing trends.

With this type of enthusiasm for the magazine, you might guess the type of anticipation I have had for this new book. I am honored to have *Sew News Timesaving Tips* as part of the "Sewing With Nancy" book series.

Sew News Editor Linda Griepentrog and her staff have done an excellent job of gathering and organizing prime tips from stimulating articles that have appeared over the years. This easy-to-use book will help us get organized, use notions to make sewing easier, incorporate designer shortcuts, create with our serger, sew functional and creative closures, and take care of our garments and fabric—an often overlooked topic. I know that you and I will refer to this book nearly every time we sew.

Thanks, *Sew News!*

Nancy Zieman

INTRODUCTION

Linda Turner Griepentrog
Editorial Director, Editor

Time — nobody seems to have enough of it, and there's no way to add to our daily 24-hour allotment. The solution is to work smarter. There are always different ways to accomplish the same task, and as sewers we want to choose the one that best uses our time. So we have filled *Sew News Timesaving Tips* with sewing shortcuts designed to save you time and energy without sacraficing results.

We hope that our book will find a comfortable place in your sewing room, and using these ideas will allow you to spend more time doing what you love most—sewing.

Annette Bailey
Managing Editor/Fashion

Laurie Baker
Assistant Editor/Fabric

Carol Zentgraf
Assistant Editor/New Products

Sue Barnabee
Special Projects Coordinator

About *Sew News...* *Sew News* began publication in the fall of 1980, the brainchild of two Seattle women, Laura Rehrmann and Robin Siegl, who loved sewing and wanted to share that passion. The magazine quickly grew, and in 1983 *Sew News* was purchased by PJS Publications and moved to its current home in Peoria, Illinois.

THE MAGIC CLOAK

We've all done it—

fallen in love with a fabric on sight and bought it with no idea how we would use it. Rather than store the fabric away in a closet while you decide its fate, try making the Magic Cloak. It's magic because it doesn't limit the future use of your fabric—since you never cut.

Materials

• 2½ yards of fabric (36"-wide fabric makes a knee-length garment, depending on the wearer's height, and 45"-wide fabric makes a full-length garment)
• Matching thread

Construction

1. Hem the cut edges of the fabric or finish with decorative serger stitching, fringing, or binding.

2. With right sides together and finished edges matching, stitch a 9" seam beginning at the upper selvage edge. The shorter the first seam, the smaller will be the difference between the front and back lengths. Press open.

Sew a 9"-long seam.

3. Refold the fabric to center the 9" seam, and match the selvage upper edges.

4. Begin stitching 10" from one folded end and stitch the selvages together. Stop stitching 10" from the remaining folded edge. The unstitched sections will form the armholes.

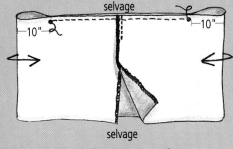

Refold and sew selvages together.

5. Turn the cloak right side out, place the finished edges around your neck, and insert your arms through the 10" openings.

Variations

Be sure the Magic Cloak does not cling to the outfit you are wearing underneath. Adjust the cloak until it feels comfortable. If the fabric does not drape well, use a belt to achieve a look you like. Roll the "lapels" to the outside or inside.

If the fabric you've purchased is very sheer, or if you're using more than 2½ yards, run a basting stitch along the selvage seam. Gather to approximately 18". Now try on the cloak and adjust the gathers so the garment feels comfortable; then restitch the gathered area to stabilize it.

If you decide not to use the fabric of the Magic Cloak for another project, you can be a bit more creative. Apply trims, tucks, or pleats, and hem the cloak to a desired length.

Uses for the Magic Cloak

• When you need a party outfit at the last minute, choose a spectacular fabric and wear it over basic black.
• Wear the cloak as a robe when you've lowered the thermostat to conserve energy. The hem is shorter in the front, making it easier to walk in than some longer robes.
• Select gorgeous fabric for a fancy maternity "dress." You'll be able to turn it into a party dress next year.
• Make a terry cloth cloak; use as a swimsuit cover-up and a beach towel.
• Scale the cloak down for children—it makes a great first sewing project.

GETTING
ORGANIZED

Number one sewing timesaver—

getting (and keeping) yourself organized.

Learn to make good purchasing decisions, create an efficient

room layout, ban clutter, and consciously plan

before you sew to make the best use of your precious time.

SEWING ROOM ORGANIZATION

The dream of every fashion sewer is to have a spacious sewing room

with everything right at your fingertips. And even though we have to make do with

what we have, with advance planning and special attention to setup, lighting,

and storage, almost everyone can have a functional work space.

Room to sew

Your first task is to determine where you'll set up shop. Regardless of where you locate your sewing space, it should be efficient and comfortable; tools and materials should be within easy reach; and if the space is to be shared with other activities, you should be able to put things away quickly or keep them hidden.

Of course, an entire room devoted solely to sewing is probably your dream, but if you can't find that much space, consider the following options, keeping in mind that if space is limited, you can store fabrics and patterns somewhere else in the house.

Convert a closet

You might be surprised to know that a standard 2'x5' closet provides enough space for a sewing machine and storage (see figure). All the necessities will be within reach. And when you're finished sewing, you can simply close the door. Begin your closet renovation by taking some preliminary steps (see box).

Easy closet renovation

- Paint the interior white to add a clean look and the illusion of space.
- If your closet has sliding doors, replace them with bifolds or swing doors so the entire area will be accessible when you're sewing.
- Install a work surface, such as a Formica™ kitchen countertop.
- Add shelving above the work surface. Standard 8' ceilings will accommodate three or four shelves; 10' ceilings allow for five shelves.
- Roll a wire basket or stacked drawer unit under the sewing table to hold notions, tools and patterns.
- Hang a mirror, pegboard or bulletin board on the back of a standard door, or face the entire door with cork. You can even hinge another work surface to the door for added sewing space. When the door is open, the table can drop down, supported by legs or a stacked drawer unit.

swing doors

shelving

rolling carts with baskets

pegboard

bulletin board

Sewing closet

Put a short wall to work

Use a short wall to accommodate a large table for your sewing surface. Think about the bedroom, guest room, kitchen, laundry room, or a small hallway alcove. With the table as your base, you can extend your sewing area up the wall and outward, making use of a wall-mounted ironing board and rolling carts with baskets.

Sewing wall

Divide a room

Bookcases and folding screens make excellent
dividers. They can hide your sewing space from the
rest of the room.

bookcase divider

folding screen

Sewing room

Setting up

Divide your work area regardless of its size into three activity areas: 1) layout and cutting, 2) sewing and 3) pressing. Consider these three areas as workstations. The U-shape setup, which features the sewing machine placed between the pressing area and a side work area for pinning, basting, handwork or serging, is generally the best arrangement. The L-shape arrangement, with the sewing table at a right angle to your other work space, is the next best choice. Working right to left is typical, but left to right may be more comfortable for you. Placement of your equipment will depend on your work patterns. Keep in mind that if you have to reach too far or bend at awkward angles over long periods of time, neck or back injuries may result.

Layout and cutting area

You can mount a cutting surface on top of a chest, a cabinet, or two sets of pull-out wire basket units. For cutting ease, position the surface so you can walk around at least three sides. The height will depend on your own height and leg length, but it should be around 36". The ideal cutting surface is approximately 36"x72" to allow you to cut any fabric width (folded if necessary), but the surface can be as small as 30"x36". An island workstation is best, provided there is enough room to walk around it. When choosing or building an island, make sure it is the correct height and has storage shelves or drawers underneath.

If space is limited, you may want to consider a portable table that you can put away after use, or a more permanent surface, such as the dining room table, that you can convert into a cutting area.

sewing area

pressing area

multipurpose side work area—use for layout and cutting as well as serging

The U-shape work setup

Another option is to create a cut-and-press board as follows:

1. Pad the cutting surface (a board) ½" to ¾" thick with cotton upholstery wadding or wool fabric.

2. Tightly wrap heavy cotton twill or special cloth with grid markers over the surface top and around its sides.

3. Use an upholstery hammer and tacks or a staple gun to fasten the fabric to the underside.

You can mount this cut-and-press board on a wall for easy storage, but remember that because of its weight, it will require the support of legs or a storage unit when in use.

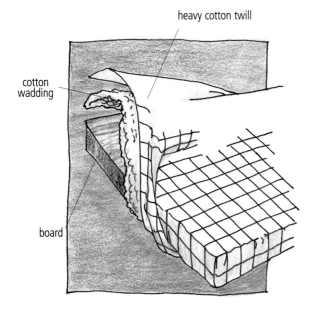

Cut-and-press board

Pressing area

You can do your pressing on the cut-and-press board mentioned above or on an ironing board. The advantage to the ironing board is that it can be adjusted to seat height (24") for timesaving stitch-and-press sewing.

✉ **Note:** If you don't have space for a traditional ironing board, use a wall-mounted board, which can be folded up and out of the way, or try a portable ironing board.

Sewing area

The sewing and serging area should provide enough space to support your fabric and allow you to maneuver it. There should be at least 24" between the sewing machine and serger for easy work flow. To avoid neck and back injuries while sewing, position your machine beds approximately 28" from the floor. If possible, put your machines at right angles so you'll need only to turn your chair to move from one to the other. If you must place the machines side by side, put a chair in front of each or use an office chair with wheels to save time when moving back and forth.

Sewing table possibilities

• Typing table or computer desk

• Sewing center or office workstation

• Formica™ countertop supported by filing cabinets. The countertop can be cut to any length and it is easy to clean. To reduce fabric slippage while sewing, select a slightly textured countertop.

• Solid wood door or board, supported by cabinets or wire basket systems

• Unfinished desk or table, painted or stained and varnished to match your decor

• Collector's item such as an antique treadle machine cabinet to house your sewing machine, if you're an antique buff

• Cupboard or armoire that looks like furniture when it's closed. This is ideal if your sewing area shares space with other activities.

✉ **Note:** The surface heights of the alternative pieces listed may be too high or too low for sewing comfort. An adjustable office-style chair on casters will bring you to the desired height and give you stability. For an adult, the chair seat should be about 16" from the floor, when the sewing machine bed is 28" from the floor. A good chair can be expensive, but it will prevent muscle fatigue and backaches.

Lighting

Sewing requires twice as much light as casual reading. Good lighting is essential to work-space design because it reduces eyestrain and costly sewing or pressing mistakes, thus allowing you to work longer. For sewing, you'll need shadowless light directed at the sewing machine or at the work in your hands. Lighting falls into two general categories—general overhead lighting and task lighting.

General overhead lighting

For overall illumination of the room, a combination of ceiling and side lighting is perfect. Some experts recommend fluorescent fixtures with whole-spectrum bulbs to enhance all colors; others suggest using versatile track lighting. Natural lighting can serve as general lighting on sunny days, but working facing the sunlight actually causes fatigue. If the sewing center is near a window, place the equipment so the light comes in over your left shoulder if you're right-handed or over your right shoulder if you're left-handed.

Task lighting

Task lighting is close-up lighting. Gooseneck or drafting lamps clamped to your worktable are among the best options. Clamp spotlights can be mounted to overhead shelving.

> ✉ **Note:** Keep in mind that a room with white or light window treatments, walls, ceilings and floors won't absorb light or energy. A light color scheme actually helps you to sew longer without fatigue.

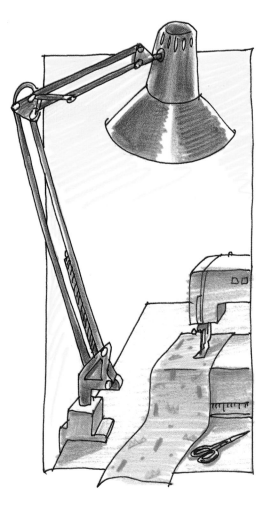

Task lighting: Use drafting lamps or clamp spotlights for close-up lighting.

Storage options

Like most sewers, you probably have stacks of fabric, patterns, and notions that need to be organized. Although this may sound like a daunting task, it will save you time in the end because everything will be easy to find. Here are some tricks to keep your supplies in order.

Fabrics

Organizing your fabric stash can be a major undertaking. You have to be brutal—give away any fabric you've stored for more than two years. For easy project planning, it's best to organize fabric by color, fiber type, or end use.

Take over a closet and install vinyl-coated shelving from floor to ceiling.
Stack folded fabrics on existing shelves wherever you can claim the space.

> ✉ **Note:** Wood shelving may damage fabric over time.

Commandeer a cupboard or armoire with shelves.
Store fabric in colorful plastic stacking crates, either in your sewing space or on a closet floor or shelf.

Plastic crates

towel bar

padded hanger

wicker basket

Fabric storage ideas

Store wools with moth crystals in a trunk or in a box under your bed.
Roll fabrics that would be harmed by creasing—silk, linen, suede or pile fabrics—onto empty fabric bolts. Store the bolts upright in a wicker basket for a colorful room accent.
Fold fabrics over padded hangers or on towel bars mounted on a closet door.

Interfacing

Roll folded interfacing yardage onto discarded cardboard tubes.

Tuck the manufacturer's instruction sheet for fusibles inside the tube for quick reference.

Place a wine rack or a crate on a shelf near your pressing surface to hold the interfacing tubes.

Use large freezer bags to hold folded interfacings. Label and file the bag in a box or filing cabinet.

Patterns

Begin by sorting through your pattern collection, eliminating outdated styles and sizes. Store the patterns you want to keep in these containers:

Cardboard pattern boxes. Available in many fabric stores, these are made specifically for pattern storage.

Filing cabinets. If you have extra room after filing your patterns, file magazine articles and other sewing ideas in the cabinets, too.

Plastic crates. These colorful, lightweight containers hold many patterns and are available at discount and office supply stores.

Empty diaper or laundry detergent boxes. Covered with fabric or self-adhesive vinyl, these provide inexpensive storage.

Cardboard file storage boxes. Look for the closet-shop variety that come in colorful patterns, or cover the standard file boxes with fabric or self-adhesive vinyl.

Cardboard file boxes

Notions

Thread, pins, needles, scissors, measuring tools and all those other little notions—how do you keep them separate and still accessible? Here are some creative yet practical ideas.

Storage racks. Place thread spools and cones on these handy racks. This works best when your sewing space is relatively dust free.

> ✉ **Note:** For timesaving selection, organize cones and spools of thread by type, then color.

Coffee cans with plastic lids. Add pocketed fabric covers for additional storage space.

Cutlery or flatware trays. The narrow compartments can hold measuring tapes, marking tools, rotary cutters, and scissors.

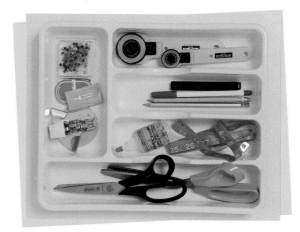

Flatware tray

Small kitchen containers with lids. Baby food jars and desk accessories are great keepers for small notions such as snaps, hooks and eyes, buttons and trims. Arrange them on a small lazy Susan for easy selection.

Metal hardware chest. In the shallow drawers, store items like thread, zippers and seam tape.

Wicker baskets. These lightweight, portable storage units hold everything from small tools to interfacing and fabric scraps.

Wicker baskets

Pegboard or wall-mounted racks. Install these behind the sewing machine to hang shallow trays or baskets, as well as single items.

Fabric pockets. Attached to the side of the sewing machine, these can hold patterns, thread snips, and other frequently used notions.

See-through hanging shoebags or roll-up lingerie cases. The clear pockets are great for keeping tools handy while sewing. Hang the bag or case in a closet when not needed.

Stackable plastic shoeboxes with lids. Use separate boxes for different notions, such as zippers, laces, trims, elastics, and tapes.

Bulletin boards. Post current information, magazine clippings, and pattern guidesheets for easy reference.

Storage containers/product dispensers

Many sewing products are packaged in blister packs—rigid plastic on a cardboard card. A blister pack displays the product well, but it can be ruined by hasty opening, which can also render the instructions on the back illegible. By following these simple steps, you can turn this type of package into a handy storage container and product dispenser with the instructions printed right on the back.

1. Carefully cut the plastic blister close to the base where it is attached to the card.

2. Extend the cut approximately halfway around the blister.

3. Remove the product to use it, and then put it back in the package for storage.

4. To make the package into a handy dispenser as well, cut a small rectangular opening in the side of the blister.

5. With your fingers or tweezers, pull the product through the opening.

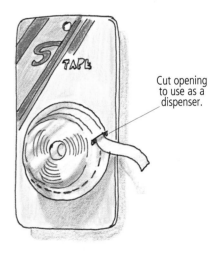

Cut opening to use as a dispenser.

Package dispenser: Store notions in their original packages.

SHOPPING WISELY

Purchasing supplies for your projects takes time, but it's one of the most important tasks to ensure success. Buying right enables you to sew right.

Mail-order mania

Shopping for fabric and notions by mail is smart, especially if you live in an area with limited selection. Mail ordering broadens your choices, and you can even shop in the middle of the night!

Successful mail-order shopping

• Read the fine print in the catalog and on the order form so you know about shipping and handling charges, delivery time, shipping options, substitutions, minimum quantities, dye lot differences, and so on.
• Keep a record of the company's name and address; date, time and method by which the order was placed; description of the items ordered, and their cost and stock numbers; total cost of the order, including shipping fees; method of payment; and the name of the person who took your order, if you called it in.
• Look carefully at the fabric swatch or catalog picture for color, fabric width, fiber content, and pattern repeat. Many companies offer personalized services with orders, such as thread or interfacing selection.
• Don't assume the worst if your order doesn't arrive when expected. Write or call the company. If you receive the wrong items, contact the customer service department.
• When requesting a catalog or other information from a mail-order company, you'll receive a quicker response if you enclose a self-addressed, stamped envelope (SASE) and send your request separately from your order. (Catalog requests and orders usually go to different departments.)

Bargain basics

If you shop for sewing supplies in off-price stores that feature sharp discounts, be sure you know what you're looking for when you read labels.

Understanding the terms below will help make you a savvy shopper.

As Is: Buyer, beware! The store isn't responsible for anything wrong with the item. Watch for holes, soil, dye flaws, and other damage.

Designer Cut: Premeasured length used by a designer to preview a line of fabric. Often a one-of-a-kind design, weave, or print.

Discontinued Item: Product that will no longer be available.

Factory Outlet: Store owned by a manufacturer and selling only that manufacturer's products at less than retail prices.

Flat Fold: Fabric not stored on a bolt. Sometimes first quality, often an overrun or mill-end.

Out-of-Season Merchandise: Leftover items from a previous season.

Sample: Usually a small-sized item originally produced for sales representatives to use in soliciting orders.

Second: Item containing a flaw, such as a hole or tear. Check carefully and decide whether you can work around the flaw.

Wise buys

Beautiful fabrics are the motivating force behind many sewing projects, yet selecting just the right fabric for a project can be a challenge. To shop for fabrics wisely, follow these four basic steps.

1. Look

• Selecting a fabric with a large motif requires pre-planning to place the motif where it is most visually appealing. You may need to purchase extra fabric to allow for this placement. Small busy prints, on the other hand, normally don't require preplanning or extra yardage, but they will hide construction details such as tucks, pleats or decorative seams.

• One-way designs also require extra fabric, because all pattern pieces must be placed on the fabric going the same direction. Examples of one-way designs include unbalanced stripes or plaids and floral prints with all stems pointed downward. The amount of extra fabric needed depends on the size of the motif, but ¼ to ½ yard extra is typical for small to medium-sized designs.

• Keep scale and proportion in mind.

• Hold the fabric up to the light and look for thin areas and irregular or broken yarns.

2. Touch

• Texture is as important as color to the appearance of the project. Shiny fabrics will reflect light, making the person appear larger. Pile fabrics or fabrics with nap, such as corduroy or velvet, absorb light, diminishing size and providing a rich, soft look.

• Fabrics reflecting light differently (such as velvet and corduroy) require a one-way, with-nap layout. If you cut pattern pieces in both directions, your finished garment will look as if it were made from different color fabrics.

• Check the degree of fabric drape. Does the fabric seem too stiff or fluid for your project?

3. Read

• The label on the fabric bolt end will usually list key information about the fabric, the manufacturer, and where the fabric was produced.

• Check the fabric care requirements and fiber content. This information will help determine not only care requirements but also construction steps.

• Note the fabric width. The amount of fabric you purchase for a given project is determined by the fabric width; the amount needed is listed on the back of the pattern envelope. If you're working with a fabric width not given on the envelope, check the conversion chart in the Appendix of this book.

4. Ask

After looking, touching and reading, ask one more question: How advanced are my skills? If you're a beginner, or beginning again after a long break, steer clear of fabrics that require special treatment.

• Pile fabrics such as corduroy or velvet require care when pressing.

• Slippery fabrics can shift during stitching.

• Plaids and stripes demand careful attention during layout, cutting, and sewing.

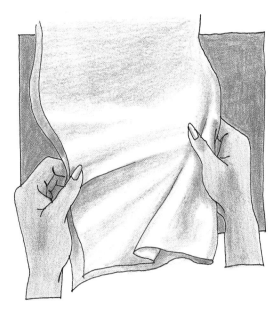

Look, touch, and read labels, and ask about sewing skill required before buying a fabric.

PREPARING FABRIC

Most of us want to get right to sewing our garments. But don't

be tempted to skip pretreating your fabric. Your investment of time and materials is

wasted if your garment shrinks the first time it's cleaned. Follow this simple rule:

pretreat the fabric as you plan to treat the garment.

Think preshrink

Despite labels that read "preshrunk" or "needle-ready," most fabrics do shrink. As fabric is rolled onto tubes or bolts at the factory, it passes through a machine under tension, which actually stretches the fabric. When you launder, clean, or press the fabric for the first time, the heat and steam cause the fabric to relax from the strain of being wrapped on the bolt. This is called relaxation shrinkage. The fabric, not the fiber, is shrinking back to its original size.

To prevent major disappointments, preshrink all components of your project before sewing. Treat the fabric according to the care instructions given on the bolt end, and pretreat project interfacings, zippers, laces, elastic, and trims in the same manner. This might mean hand washing and line drying, machine washing and drying, or dry-cleaning.

Preshrinking is only one reason for pretreating fabric; removing chemical finishes and sizing is another. These finishes often enhance texture, drape and sheen and can mislead you if the garment is fitted before the fabric is cleaned. They can also coat the machine needle, causing skipped stitches.

Determine fabric pretreatment methods by the fiber content of the fabric.

Wool

Most wools require dry-cleaning, but you may steam-shrink the fabric at home. If you're concerned about shrinkage, buy an additional ⅛ yard of fabric and have the entire piece cleaned before cutting out your garment.

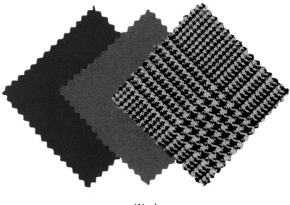

Wool

Silk

If you prewash the fabric before sewing, you'll be able to wash your silk garments. Prewashing also reduces the likelihood of later ruining the garment with a washing accident or water spots, and it saves on dry-cleaning costs.

Hand washing silk actually rejuvenates the fibers, and it produces the least amount of shrinkage and the fewest fabric changes. To compensate for minimal shrinkage, buy an extra ⅛ yard for every 2 yards of fabric you need. And test-wash a scrap before you wash the entire piece of fabric.

To help retain the silk's true color, add ¼ cup of white vinegar to every two gallons of water, wash the fabric in a mild detergent and squeeze to remove water. To dry, press the damp fabric using a hot, dry iron.

Some silks can be machine washed, and a few even machine dried. But repeated machine washing produces the most shrinkage and the most obvious change in color, sheen and fabric hand. Heavier crepe de chines will develop a softer drape and a fine, suedelike feel.

Wash the yardage by itself on a delicate cycle in cool water and mild detergent. To machine dry the fabric, choose a cool or delicate setting.

Even if you plan to dry-clean the finished garment, it's still a good idea to preshrink the silk yardage for the reasons mentioned. Although brightly colored silks will fade somewhat with dry-cleaning, the color change won't be as extensive as that produced by hand or machine washing and the fabric's shine will remain. With dry-cleaning, silk will look newer longer, even though the chemical process actually dries out the fibers, shortening the life span of the fabric and of the garment.

Synthetic blends

Blended fabrics containing more than 30% synthetic material actually shrink very little, but we recommend pretreating to remove the fabric finishes. Dry-cleaning is necessary only to control color fading or preserve delicate construction. You should dry-clean specialty fabrics such as satins, taffetas, and polyester crepes, however, to maintain color, texture and drape.

Synthetic blends

Linen

Dry-cleaning linen is preferable; machine washing tends to fade darker linens and cause the fabric to lose its crispness.

You can hand wash and line dry handkerchief linen, but you'll need to be especially careful when handling the damp fabric, as linen becomes particularly weak when wet.

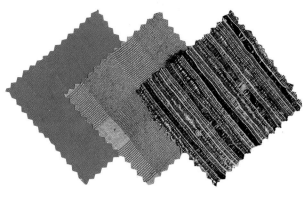

Silk

Linen

Cotton

Since cottons shrink a great deal, it's best to preshrink yardage by machine washing and drying. To allow for shrinkage, buy an extra ⅛ to ¼ yard for every 2 to 4 yards of fabric. Wash and dry the yardage at the same temperature and cycle settings you'll be using for garment care.

Cotton

Fabric fudging

Not enough fabric for your project? Tight squeeze? Turn *not-quite-enough* into *just right*.

Whether you are digging through your fabric stash or you have your heart set on a new piece of fabric to team with a great new pattern, you're sure to encounter this problem occasionally. Before you give up on the piece or the pattern, consider these ideas. While none saves yards and yards of fabric, combining several strategies can save the few inches critical to cutting a pattern out of less than the yardage listed. Planning, flexibility and ingenuity are the requirements for pattern squeezing.

Change the pattern layout

Rearrange pattern pieces. Sometimes cutting single-layer rather than double-layer can save substantial width. Folding differently can often save on fabric, as well.

Change lengthwise grainlines to crossgrain or bias on smaller pieces. Blouse and dress cuffs cut on the bias curve around the wrist more gracefully, and you often can cut these pieces from remaining odd-shaped fabric pieces.

To create a true bias grainline, fold the pattern in half with grainline matching and crease the fold. Unfold and refold on the diagonal, with the foldline on the grainline; crease. The new crease becomes the true bias grainline.

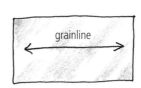

pattern

crease

Fold pattern in half; crease fold.

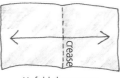

Unfold the pattern.

Refold with creased line on grainline. Crease. Crease second fold.

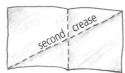

Second crease is true bias grainline.

Changing grainline to bias grainlines

Make crossgrain cuts when using stripes and plaids, eliminating some of the matching and thus saving fabric. Try this with yokes, cuff bands or pockets.

Use a contrasting fabric when cutting some pieces, such as undercollars, facings, yokes or belts.

Piece it together

Piece patterns in inconspicuous areas, like facings, undercollars, cuff folds or below jacket roll lines. Don't forget to add seam allowances to both pieced sections.

Create seams close to the hem edge to piece a widely flared skirt. Make sure you cut the pieced sections on the same grainline and add seam allowances.

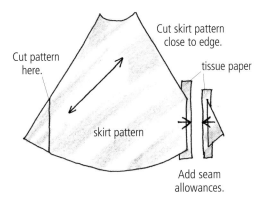

Piecing a skirt pattern

Eliminate hem and seam allowances

Shorten the pattern if possible, and make narrower hem allowances or bind or face the edges.

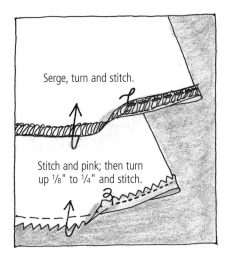

Narrowing hem allowances

Reduce seam allowances or eliminate them altogether. Any seamline that follows the straight grain can usually be cut on a fold, automatically saving 1¼" in fabric width and creating a little more wiggle room for shifting pieces in the layout.

Use the selvage as a seam finish on straight seams, such as the center back seam or the underarm sleeve seams.

Scrutinize details

Before you cut out your pattern, decide what details can be eliminated or changed to save fabric.

Eliminate full-back button closures on blouses. Change a blouse to a pull-on style by adding a center back seam allowance. Stitch the center back seam, leaving a 6" opening at the top. Narrowly hem the opening and attach the collar or facing. Add a button and loop closure at the neck edge.

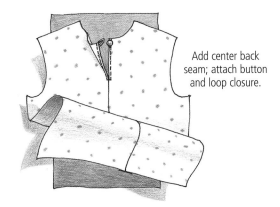

Add center back seam; attach button and loop closure.

Hemmed opening

Or cut the back on the center fold and apply a placket facing to the upper center back.

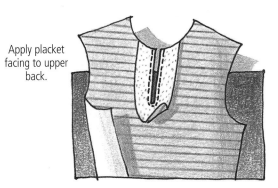

Apply placket facing to upper back.

Faced opening

Replace a button closing with a zipper, which requires no facing fabric.

Eliminate patch pockets and sew in-seam pockets in coordinating fabric.

Leave out add-on details like pockets and bands, provided this won't detract from the finished look.

Remove a little of the fullness from gathered or flared skirt styles. Take a small tuck at the hemline of the pattern piece, tapering the tuck so that it disappears below the waistline.

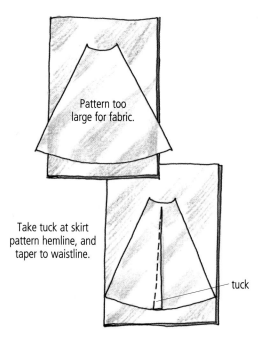

Pattern too large for fabric.

Take tuck at skirt pattern hemline, and taper to waistline.

tuck

Reducing skirt fullness

Be creative

Combine your project fabric with another fabric in a related color or print, or choose a bold, color-blocked contrast for a real work of art!

Combining fabrics

Don't stop— keep sewing

Pattern guidesheets break projects down into smaller, independent tasks, but to make the most of your sewing time, rethink the process and sew continuously. Challenge yourself to sew as many seams as you can at one time before cutting your thread. Then make a trip to press; grouping tasks saves time and energy. You can use the time you save to shop for more fabric for your next project and the next and the. . .

See how many sections of your garment you can sew consecutively without stopping or cutting apart the pieces. For example, here's how to assemble your favorite T-shirt in less than 20 minutes.

Quick T-shirt assembly

1. Stitch (or serge) the front and back together at the side seam, across one shoulder, then the second shoulder and down the remaining side seam.
2. Continue by sewing the two sleeve underarm seams, joining the ribbing seams in the neckband, waistband and two sleeve bands.
3. Between sections, simply pull extra thread or chain as needed.
4. At this point, your sewn "train" may be reaching the floor behind your sewing machine, so stop to clip the pieces apart. To complete the shirt, insert the sleeves and attach the ribbing bands.

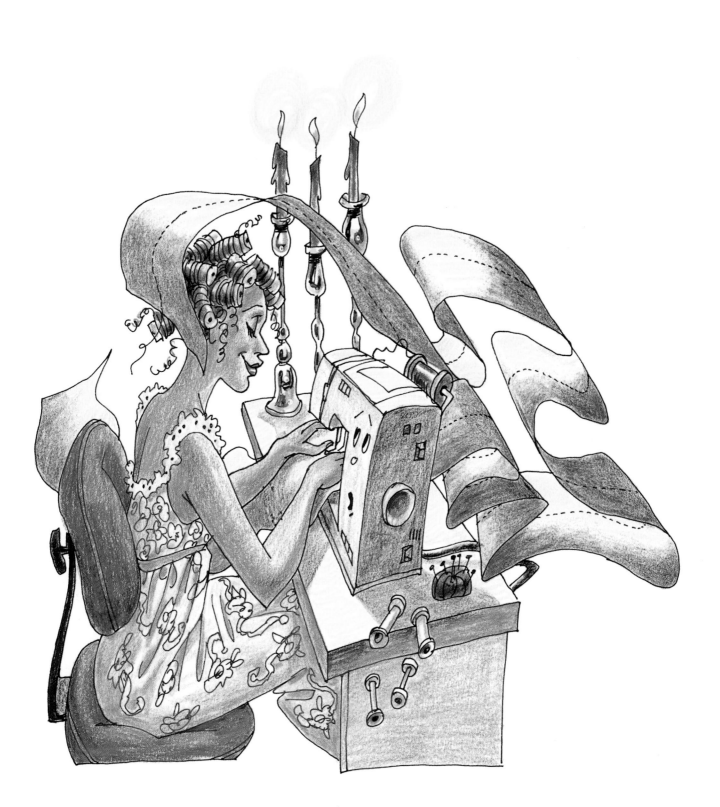

No matter what, keep sewing!

GREAT
NOTIONS

The creativity and resourcefulness

of fashion sewers around the world have produced an

abundance of great sewing notions.

T I M E S A V I N G
N O T I O N S

Whether geared toward cutting or pressing, shaping or stabilizing, these new tools make sewing easier and more fun and save valuable time. Look for these products at your local fabric and craft store. If they are not available in your area, check the source list in the Appendix for mail-order suppliers.

Cutting tools

Rotary Cutting Guide

How do you figure out what width to cut the fabric strips to fit various sizes of bias tape makers? Try the Rotary Cutting Guide for tape makers.

This new see-through ruler has five measurements to correspond with the five sizes of tape makers—¼", ½", ¾", 1", and 2"—plus convenient 45-degree bias lines. Whether you want straight-grain or bias fabric strips, this tool helps speed the measuring and cutting process.

To use, determine the finished width of the binding you want and the size tape maker you'll be using. For example, for a ⅛" finished binding, you'll need the narrowest ¼"-wide (6mm) tape maker; and a 1" finished binding requires the widest 2" (50mm) tape maker. Then select the

measuring line on the Rotary Cutting Guide according to the size tape maker you're using, and cut your fabric strips.

Strips Ahoy™ 100

Stripping takes on new meaning with this notion! Use it as a cutting guide to create fabric strips for confetti jackets, fabric rugs, corded baskets, and pin-weaving projects or for any project needing narrow strips.

This tool is composed of two layers: a lower cutting mat and an upper, clear plastic, ruled template. The template features slots so you can cut strips from ½" to 18" wide (in ½" increments), as well as 45- and 60-degree angle lines.

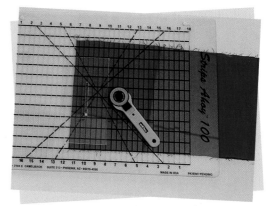

To use the cutting tool, determine the desired grain of the strips (lengthwise, crosswise, or bias), and then fold the fabric and place it between the cutting mat and template. Using a rotary cutter, cut in the center of each desired slot. As you cut, the guide holds the fabric firmly between the surfaces, allowing you to cut multiple layers of fabric at one time.

Even Cut™

Save measuring and marking time with the Even Cut, an ingenious sewing tool that allows you to measure and cut in one easy step. The Even Cut consists of a ⅝"-wide holder and a 6"-long sewing gauge. To use:

1. Mount the holder on the upper scissor blade (right blade on right-handed scissors; left blade on left-handed scissors).

2. Line up the edge of the holder along the pattern seamline to add a ⅝" seam allowance when cutting out a garment.

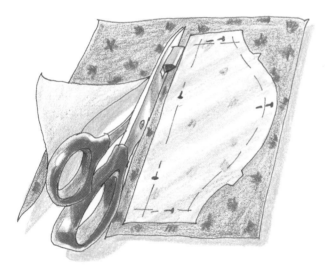

Even Cut

To use with sewing gauge:

1. Insert the sewing gauge zero edge into the Even Cut holder for a cutting guide up to 6" wide. Position the red marker at the desired cutting width less ¼" to allow for the scissors and holder. For cutting items such as ruffles, waistbands, and bias fabric strips, line up the marker along the fabric edge. To even a hem allowance, line up the marker along the hem foldline.

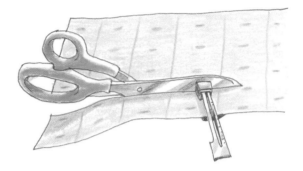

Even Cut with sewing gauge attached

2. For the most accurate cutting, use short, smooth strokes and keep your eye on the holder edge or red marker.

When not in use, the Even Cut holder stays on the scissors without interfering with other cutting jobs and the removable sewing gauge stores with other small notions.

SlipNots™

Use SlipNots, made of a self-adhesive, rubberlike material, on the back of rotary cutting rulers and templates to keep them from shifting when marking and cutting.

You can also use them to line the inside of quilter's clips to prevent the fabric from slipping. SlipNots won't snag fabric or scratch furniture.

To use, cut the SlipNots into the desired size and shape. For rulers and templates, cut a small ⅜" square or punch a dot using a ¼" paper punch; for quilter's clips, cut a narrow ¼" strip. Remove the protective paper backing and place the SlipNots in position. For best adhesion, round the corners as you cut; and place the SlipNots near the outer edges of your ruler or template to keep it from wobbling.

Tapes and stabilizers

Fusible Roll Line Tape

Tailor a wool shawl collar, notched collar and lapel, or cardigan jacket the timesaving way with Fusible Roll Line Tape. When fused in place, this ⅜"-wide stabilizer tape holds the garment snugly to the body to prevent gapping in the bust

area. It also keeps this bias area from stretching during wearing and dry-cleaning and gives the lapel the look of hours of traditional hand-tailoring.

To use Fusible Roll Line Tape:

1. Interface the garment front and mark the roll line.

2. With the interfacing side up, place the tape along the marked line, approximately ⅛" to ¼" from the mark, toward the armhole. Pin at the neck edge.

3. Mark the tape and the garment at the break point (where the roll line stops at the garment front edge).

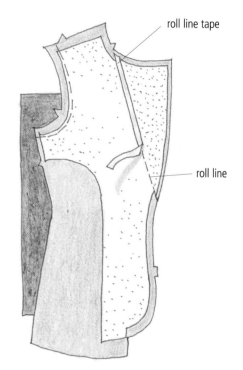

Shape lapel with Fusible Roll Line Tape.

The key to the success of steam easing when tailoring wool is to shorten the tape and ease the fabric to the tape. For an A or B bra cup or for a man's jacket, mark the tape ⅜" above the first mark; for a C or D bra cup, mark ½"; and for larger cup sizes, mark ⅝".

> ✉ **Note:** Because pressing shrinks the fabric, this easing technique works only on natural-fiber fabrics.

Match the second mark on the tape to the seam-line on the garment. Pin together and trim excess tape even with the front edge. Press the ends of the tape to secure them. Then distribute the excess fabric so that the greatest amount of ease is in the center of the tape and over the bust area. For a man's jacket, distribute the ease over the chest area. Fuse the tape in place using a lift-and-lower motion; the excess ease will shrink and disappear.

Straight-Tape™

For perfect topstitching every time, reach for Straight-Tape. This tape is accurate and easy to use and helps ensure straight, even stitching of zippers, collars, pockets, welts, and garment edges—without time-consuming marking or pinning.

Straight-Tape is a 1"-wide transparent tape with a special adhesive backing that won't leave a residue on the needle. It's printed with solid colored lines ¼" apart that are perforated for precise tearing. Between the solid lines are silver marks to aid in positioning the tape for stitching along ⅛" increments.

To use, simply cut Straight-Tape the length of the area to be stitched. Peel off the protective paper on the back of the tape, and place the tape on the fabric. Stitch directly through the tape, fold it along the stitching line, and carefully remove it.

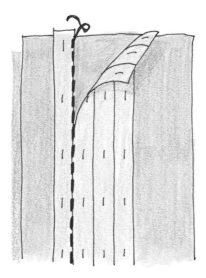

Remove tape after stitching.

If you prefer, you can stitch along the Straight-Tape edge instead. Use it at full width for a 1" topstitching guideline, or separate it along the perforations into ¼", ½", or ¾" strips.

Perfect Sew™

If you've spent time pressing stabilizer onto fabric and stretching it in a hoop to eliminate every last pucker, you'll love Perfect Sew, a wash-away liquid fabric stabilizer. This product puts an end to problem puckers and distorted designs; and it will save you valuable time when monogramming, making buttonholes, or doing any decorative stitching.

To use, simply saturate the area to be stabilized with Perfect Sew and let it dry. Perfect Sew penetrates the fabric, leaving it firm with a paperlike feel. Press with a dry iron to remove any wrinkles and you're ready to sew. When you have finished stitching, rinse the project under warm running water. Nontoxic, nonallergenic, and environmentally safe, Perfect Sew washes away completely, making it an ideal stabilizer for any type of washable fabric—from filmy sheers to stretchy knits.

Hot Tape™

Made to withstand the heat of an iron for up to five minutes, this ⅝"-wide adhesive tape can be used instead of pins for holding transfers, appliqués, trims, and ribbons in position while fusing.

Hot Tape is printed with ¼" markings like a tape measure, which makes it ideal for measuring and pressing pleats and tucks. It's great for keeping a hem allowance in place while pressing, and it's especially suitable for delicate fabrics such as silks or satins, which can be damaged easily by pinholes. Reusable Hot Tape holds securely even under the hottest iron temperature. After pressing, it peels off easily without leaving a sticky residue on your fabric or iron.

Measure and press pleats and tucks.

Hold and press hems.

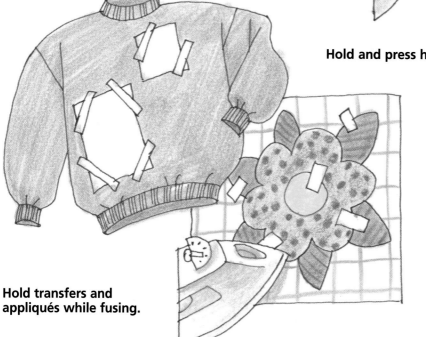

Hold transfers and appliqués while fusing.

Heat-Away™ Brush Off Stabilizer

Machine artists love the versatility of Heat-Away. Developed originally for creating cutwork and Battenberg lace, this see-through, firmly woven fabric is infused with a nontoxic chemical that causes it to disintegrate when heated.

Heat-Away is great for use as a pattern and stitching guide as well as a base fabric and stabilizer.

To use Heat-Away as a pattern or stitching guide, place the pattern design under it and trace with an extra-fine permanent marker.

Use Heat-Away as a pattern.

To use Heat-Away as a stabilizer, place it under the design area to be stitched.

Stabilize any fabric for embellishing.

If working with a looped fabric, like terry cloth, or a knit fabric, first trace the design on Heat-Away; then place it *on top* of the design area to prevent the stitches from becoming lost in the knit and the loops from distorting the stitching.

After stitching is complete, remove Heat-Away by pressing with a dry, hot iron until the stabilizer turns brown; then gently brush it away with a clean, soft-bristled toothbrush. If working with a delicate fabric or a decorative thread that could be damaged by high heat, use a press cloth and a lower iron temperature.

Remove Heat-Away by pressing.

You can also use Heat-Away as a base fabric for shaping and stitching openwork lace designs.

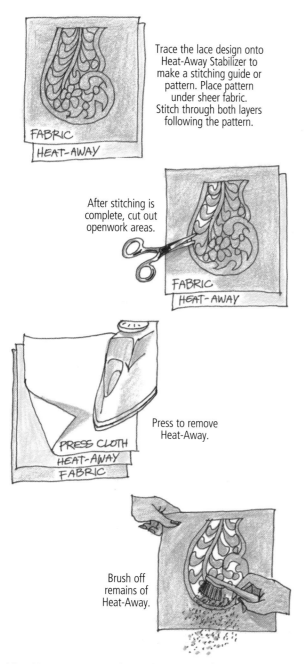

Trace the lace design onto Heat-Away Stabilizer to make a stitching guide or pattern. Place pattern under sheer fabric. Stitch through both layers following the pattern.

After stitching is complete, cut out openwork areas.

Press to remove Heat-Away.

Brush off remains of Heat-Away.

Use Heat-Away as base for cutwork.

✉ **Note:** Test Heat-Away on a fabric scrap. Also, make certain that there is no water in the iron and that water or moisture does not come in contact with Heat-Away while it's attached to your fabric. Moisture could cause the chemical in Heat-Away to dissolve and permeate the fabric, which would then disintegrate when heated.

Needles and pins

Diamond Eye Needle™

For some people, threading a needle can be a difficult and time-consuming sewing task.

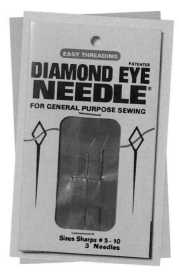

The Diamond Eye Needle is a general-purpose hand-sewing needle with a very fine, diamond-shaped wire at the end that makes threading easy. Just place the thread through the wire, and you're ready to sew. When you stitch, the flexible wire collapses to slip easily through the fabric without marring or distorting it. The needle then returns to its original size and shape.

Diamond Eye Needle

The Diamond Eye Needle is also handy for mending snags. Position the needle on the right side of the fabric at the point of the snag. Push the needle through the fabric up to the wire and then slip the snagged thread into the wire eye. Pull the needle through to the fabric wrong side.

Appliqué Pins

Timesaving aptly describes these tiny pins. They measure a mere ½" in length and virtually eliminate the frustrating and time-consuming problem of the

thread tangling around dressmaker pins as you sew.

Appliqué Pins are great for basting basic shapes and pinning curves, points, and intricate designs. Place several pins in a small area to secure your fabric; they won't get in the way of each other or catch the thread while you sew. Designed for holding appliqué pieces to the background fabric, Appliqué Pins also work well for positioning delicate laces used in heirloom and lingerie sewing.

Secure fabric and laces with Appliqué Pins.

Quilt-Safe Curved Basting Pins

Many quilting experts recommend using safety pins when basting a quilt together, especially when machine quilting. Safety pins are quick and easy to insert, and they don't poke you or fall out as you quilt. Quilt-Safe Curved Basting Pins improve upon the traditional safety pin. Made of nickel-plated brass, these pins are rustproof and can be left safely in the quilt for as long as the stitching process takes. The small 1¹⁄₁₆" length (size 1) holds the quilt layers securely and prevents them from shifting during quilting. The unique curved feature makes the pins easier to insert and close and helps keep the quilt flat.

Place pins 2" to 5" apart, depending on the type of batting used. To streamline the process, open all the pins before you begin pinning. Start at the quilt center and pin-baste to the edges, avoiding quilting design lines. Remove the pins as you quilt.

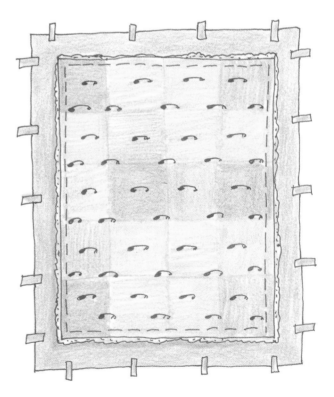

Baste a quilt with curved safety pins.

Button-Ons™

Create jewelry in an instant with Button-Ons—snap-in, snap-out button converters. Designed for use with regular shank-style buttons, these unique notions can be used for pins, earrings, bracelets, and necklaces.

The secret behind making these quick, one-of-a-kind creations is a double prong with a small wire spring of medical-grade surgical steel. Just squeeze the prongs together to snap the converter easily into the button shank. Once through the shank, the prongs expand, holding the button securely in position. With the Button-Ons converters, the button shank remains intact with no tedious gluing. Because the button isn't attached permanently to the converter, you can remove it and use both Button-Ons and button over and over again.

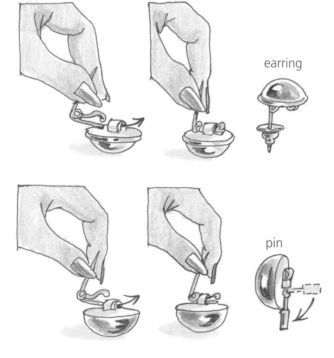

earring

pin

Earring and pin made with Button-Ons

Sewing and fitting guides

Heirloom Stitcher's Shape 'N Press™ board

If heirloom sewing, with its ruffles, frills, and elegant details, is part of your sewing scheme, you're sure to welcome the Heirloom Stitcher's Shape 'N Press board. Created to save time when shaping lace, blocking puffing strips, or pinning pleated fabric to size for smocking, this portable pressing surface actually does double duty. The convenient 14"x20" size makes it ideal to keep by the sewing machine for pressing construction details.

Made of sturdy muslin and foam-covered fiberboard, this two-sided pressing surface features red 1" grid lines on both sides to help ensure grain-perfect pressing. For shaping lace, one side of the board is printed with multisized heirloom templates: teardrop, diamond, heart, scallop, and loop. The reverse side of the board has rule markings on all four edges of the grid, as well as a Bishop template and collar smocking guide in six sizes, ranging from newborn to adult.

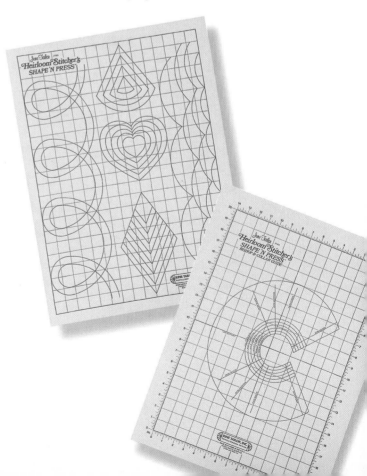

Multiple Cording Guide

As the popularity of embellishing with decorative stitching continues to grow, so does frustration with tangled threads. The more threads you use, the greater chance there is for tangling. The Multiple Cording Guide is a simple yet effective notion that can take care of this problem.

The Multiple Cording Guide is a translucent, flexible plastic tool with five thread-guide holes and a center positioning hole. When put in front of the pintuck or cording foot, it ensures that multiple threads or cords stay in proper alignment and prevents them from changing position or twisting.

Use the guide on straight or curved lines for many design possibilities. To add greater textural interest and definition to stitching, for example, place several threads or cords in each hole (a threading loop is included with each guide); for a wider band of decorative stitching, sew several rows side by side.

Mönster Papper

Since fitting tops most sewers' lists of concerns, Mönster Papper may be just what you need to tame your sewing misfits. In Swedish, *Mönster* means pattern and *Papper* is paper. This lightweight, nonwoven fabric is available in the U.S. and will help you create fitting shells, draft patterns, and make templates for personalized designs.

Since Mönster Papper is translucent, you can trace your pattern and design markings onto it with a pencil or ballpoint pen.

The paper is strong so you can cut it and sew it together. But Mönster Papper is also soft and drapable so you can test the pattern fit accurately and make adjustments. And you will find there's no annoying static cling.

> **Note:** For easier alterations, stitch the fitting shell together with an average stitch length and loosened upper tension. When you have the perfect fit, pull out the stitching and transfer the alterations to your pattern.

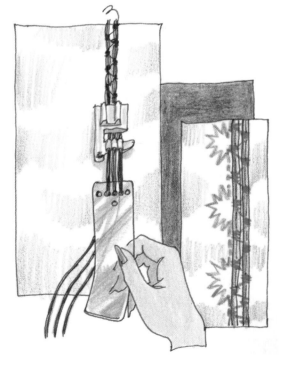

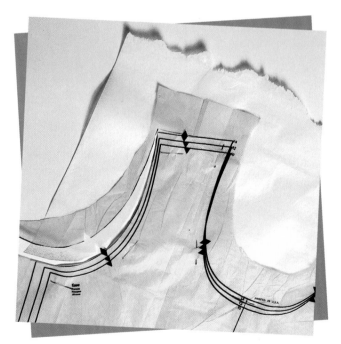

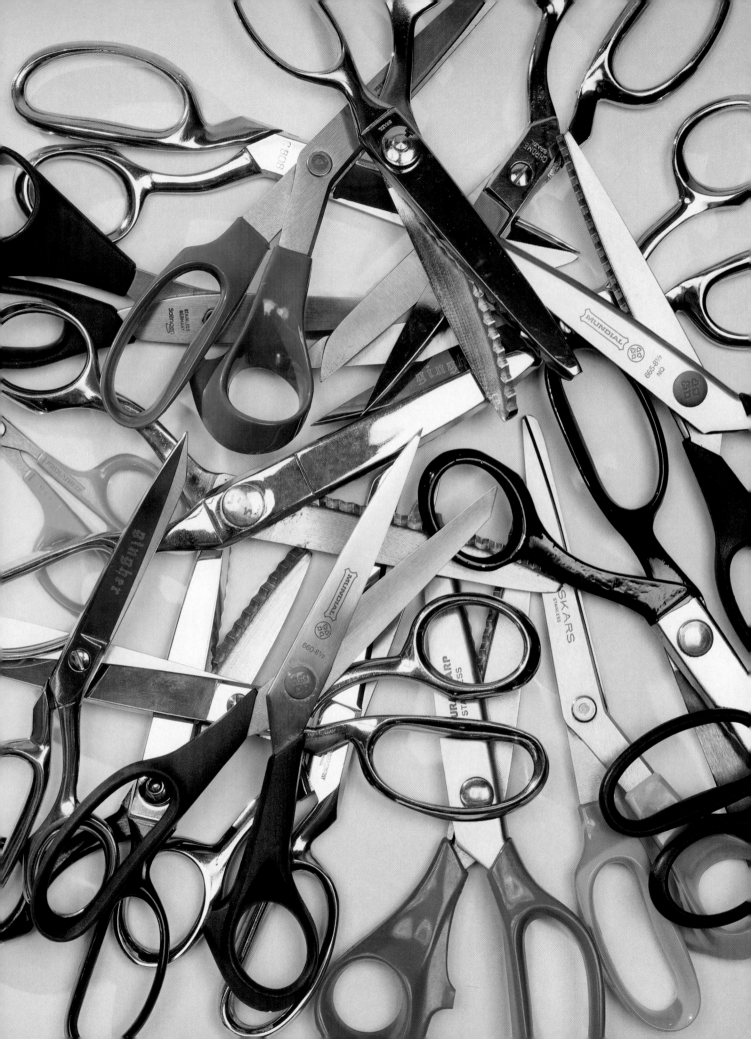

DESIGNER
SHORTCUTS

For fast yet fabulous results,

try the sewing shortcuts the designers use. You'll be

making every sewing minute count.

QUICK TRICKS

Borrow simple tricks from designer workrooms to use

in your sewing room. You'll save time and money

on every project you make.

Bias busters

Creating your own bias tape allows you to add a personal touch to garments, whether that tape is used for binding edges, seam finishes, or decorative trimming. With this quick-and-easy method for making bias tape, you'll think of using tape more often.

Binding edges

Quick-and-easy bias tape

1. Cut and stitch the bias strips to the required width and length and trim one end diagonally.

2. Secure a straight pin to the edge of your ironing board by inserting the pin into the cover twice. Leave a distance equal to the width of the finished folded tape between the two insertions. For wide strips, use T-pins or flower pins.

3. With wrong side up, work the diagonal end of the bias strip under the pin center for about 2". The raw edges of the strip will automatically roll to the center. Adjust the strip so that the folds are even and the edges are smooth; press.

4. Gently pull the strip through the pin for another 3" or so; press. Continue pulling and pressing along the entire length of the tape.

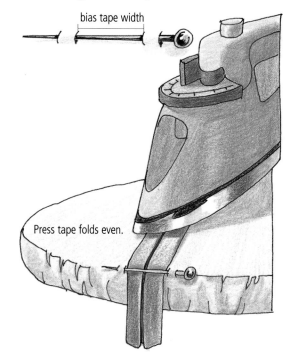

Press tape folds even.

bias tape width

Making bias tape

On your mark

Use soap to transfer markings from patterns to washable fabrics. You'll never have to worry about removing the marks—they'll either press out or disappear after the first wash.

Collect travel-size soaps from hotels and airlines and whittle one end to a sharp edge for accurate marking. Or, as soap slivers become too thin for use in the shower, recycle them from the bathroom to the sewing room.

Hidden agenda

An attractive detail used by noted designers Christian Dior and Cristobal Balenciaga is the in-seam buttonhole, which can be added to almost any pattern. The technique saves the time and tedium of stitching button loops or

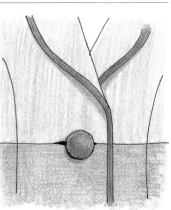

In-seam buttonhole

bound buttonholes. These buttonholes are usually found in the seam joining a band to the bodice or skirt, a collar or bodice seam, or a yoke seam. Garments using this buttonhole technique are lined or faced so the wrong side is finished attractively.

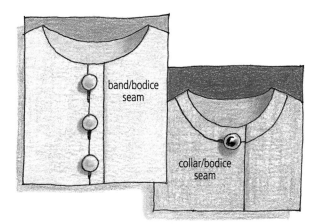

band/bodice seam

collar/bodice seam

In-seam buttonhole positions

Modifying the pattern

If the pattern doesn't have a seamline where you would like to add in-seam buttonholes, follow these steps:

1. Draw the new seamline on the pattern. Mark the buttonhole position on the new seamline and mark the grainlines on both sections.

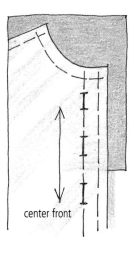

center front

Add new seamline.

2. Cut the pattern on the new seamlines, and add ⅝" seam allowances to both sections. Repeat the process to add a corresponding seamline to the facing or lining.
3. To reduce the bulk, replace the seamline at the garment edge with a foldline to incorporate the new band with the facing.

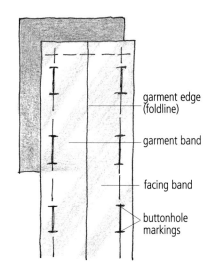

garment edge (foldline)

garment band

facing band

buttonhole markings

Combine garment band with facing band.

4. Cut out the garment. Snip-mark the buttonhole ends on the edges of the band.

5. Cut several ⅜"-wide fusible interfacing strips. To reinforce the band or bodice seam, fuse interfacing strips to the adjoining seam of each section, aligning the interfacing edges with the seam allowance.

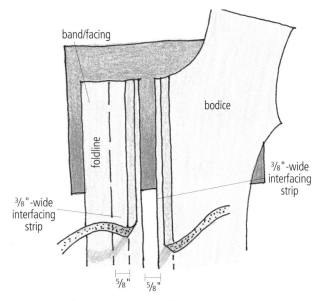

Fuse interfacing to seam allowances.

6. With right sides together, stitch the seam, backstitching carefully at the beginning and end of each buttonhole. Press the seams open.

7. To finish the buttonholes, slipstitch the garment buttonhole to the facing or lining buttonhole.

Dart-smart pointers

Stitching the perfect point at the end of a dart is a challenge for even the most experienced fashion sewer. There's always a chance of a little bubble or pucker at the tip to label the garment as homemade. Tying the thread ends is too time consuming. Try these knotless methods for point perfection:

Reverse antics

1. Stitch from the widest to the narrowest end of the dart and stop.

2. Raise the needle out of the fabric, lift the presser foot, and carefully reinsert the needle in the stitching line about ⅜" behind the dart point.

3. Stitch to the point of the dart again, directly on top of the first line of stitching.

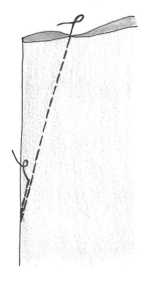

Double-stitch to secure.

Short takes

1. Stitch the dart from the widest to the narrowest point. When you're about 1" from the tip, shorten the stitch length to 20 stitches per inch.

2. Stitch off the fabric fold; secure the thread ends with a liquid seam sealant.

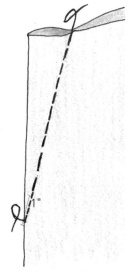

Shorten stitch length to secure.

Striped to a T

Perplexed by stripes as you sew a seam? To save time and aggravation and ensure perfect stripe alignment every single time, look to your knitting friends for help.

Blocking pins—sturdy two-pronged pins used for blocking knitted yardage—are perfect for holding stripes in place for seaming. And the colorful plastic heads make removing them a snap!

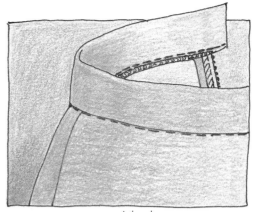
waistband

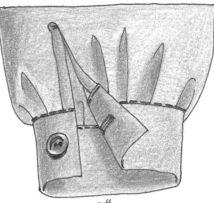
cuff

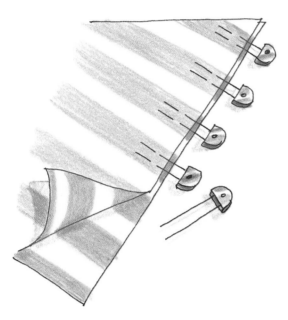

Blocking pins

Stitching in-the-ditch

If the only reason you stitch in-the-ditch is to tack facings in place, you're probably spending a lot of time doing hand sewing that could be done by machine. Stitching in-the-ditch not only saves time; it also helps you achieve a professional look.

Eliminate much of your time-consuming hand-stitching by stitching in-the-ditch to attach the inner edge of waistbands, cuffs, and straight-band collars. Use a selvage or serged edge for single-layer finishing, or turn under or bind the raw edges before stitching.

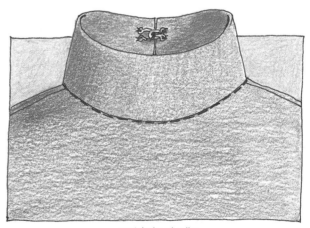
straight-band collar

Stitching in-the-ditch

For lined jackets, use stitch-in-the-ditch techniques to hold the hem up at center back, side back, and side front seams. This will work only on lined jackets with at least five lengthwise seams—or on lined two-piece jacket sleeves. For best results, stitch in-the-ditch by beginning ⅛" or more from the hem fold and ending ¼" from the hem raw edge.

If you plan to topstitch your jacket collar and lapels, stitch in-the-ditch as you turn the corner from the collar to the lapel.

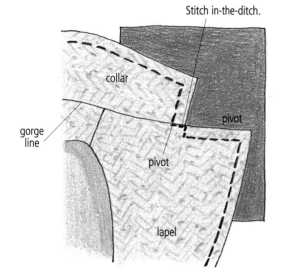

Jacket collar and lapel

If you fight twisted elastic or uneven fullness in waistband casings, stitch in-the-ditch at the side and center seams to hold the elastic in place and distribute the fullness evenly.

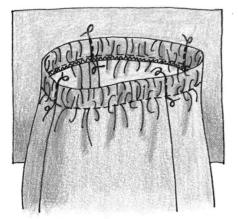

Elastic and waistbands

Hong Kong finish

Stitch in-the-ditch in a special seam finish called the Hong Kong finish. It's super for today's easy, unlined jackets.

1. Cut 1"-wide bias strips from lining fabric. Using a ¼" seam allowance, stitch to each seam edge right side. Don't stretch the bias as you stitch.

2. Wrap the bias strip around the seam allowance raw edge and stitch in-the-ditch through the bias and seam allowance only.

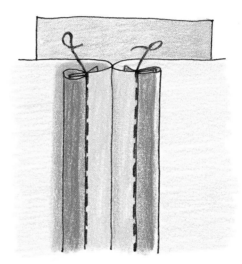

Hong Kong finish

When stitching in-the-ditch:

• Stitch from the garment right side, never from the wrong side.
• Use short stitches, at least 12 per inch.
• Match the thread so the stitching won't show on the outside.
• Use a clear plastic presser foot or the zipper foot if it's difficult to see the well of the seam when sewing. Adjust the needle position to the right or left to keep the stitching in the correct place.
• Stitching is less likely to show on soft, thick fabrics like woolens, knits, or tweeds.
• Don't backstitch—secure the stitching with seam sealant, or pull the threads to the inside and then tie off.

Gather easy

The easiest way to gather a long fabric strip or a bulky fabric is to place a heavy cord (buttonhole twist, crochet cord, or pearl cotton) just inside the seamline and zigzag over it with a long, wide stitch. Be careful not to catch the cord in the stitching, or this method won't work!

Knot one cord end to secure, and pull on the remaining end to gather. Adjust the gathers to distribute fullness evenly, and secure the remaining cord end.

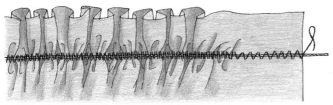

Gathering over cord

Combine several rows of corded gathers on the garment yoke, sleeves, or bodice to achieve a smocked look. Catch the knotted cord ends securely in seaming.

Cleaning up

Clean-finishing means keeping exposed fabric edges—like those at the hem, casing, or seamline raw edges—from raveling. Modern sewing technology makes it possible to accomplish this task in a variety of timesaving ways.

Overcast the raw edge using a conventional sewing machine or serger:

• Press ¼" of the fabric raw edge under and stitch close to the raw edge.

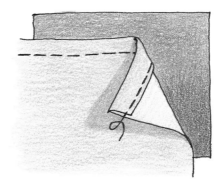

Straight-stitch finish

• Finish the fabric edge with a zigzag, multiple zigzag, or overcast-stitch on a conventional machine.

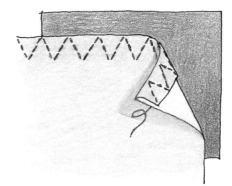

Multiple zigzag-stitch finish

• Using a serger, overcast and trim the edge simultaneously with a looped stitch.

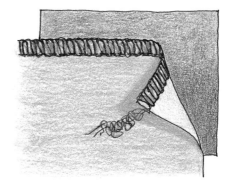

Serger finish

Pocket-proof

After stuffing your pockets with life's essentials, nothing is more frustrating than finding your pockets can't take the strain.

Anchor those corners

To avoid spending valuable sewing time mending pocket corners, try these simple reinforcement techniques used in ready-to-wear:

Use a narrow, close zigzag stitch to reinforce the corners of children's pockets. Stitch the first ½" from the upper edge of each pocket.

Zigzag corners

Backstitch blouse pockets ½" along each side of the upper edge. Bring thread ends to the wrong side and tie off.

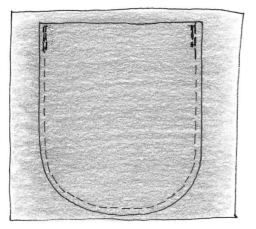

Backstitched corners

When sewing lightweight fabrics, add a small patch of fabric or fusible interfacing behind the reinforcement stitching for extra strength.

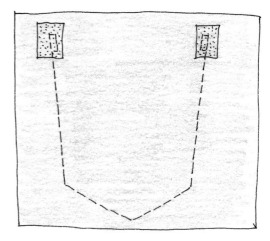

Interfacing reinforced corners

For men's tailored shirts, stitch identical triangles at each pocket corner upper edge. Backtack to anchor the threads, or bring the thread ends through to the wrong side and tie off.

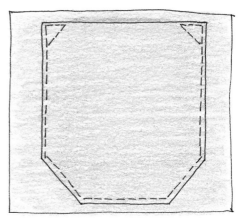

Triangle corners

To reinforce pocket corners on western designs, bartack diagonally at the upper corners with narrow, dense zigzag stitches.

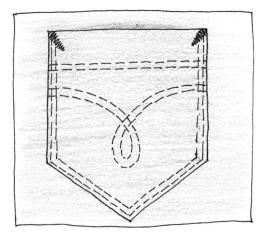

Decorative corners

Pocket pointers

Keep slanted pockets from stretching by cutting the pocket opening edge on the straight grain rather than on the bias as most instructions indicate.

The straight grain acts as a permanent stay along the pocket edge, without the bulk of stay tape. And the bias cut of the pocket bag helps it contour to the body.

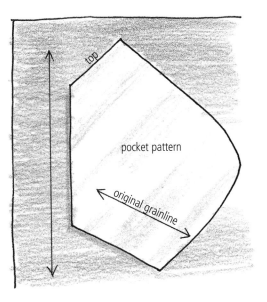

top

pocket pattern

original grainline

Cut pocket opening on lengthwise grain.

Salvage that selvage

The selvage—that narrow finished edge on woven fabrics—has many practical uses. Instead of tossing it in the trash can, put it to work as a sewing timesaver. When considering salvaging a selvage, keep in mind the following points:

Some selvages are so tightly woven that they pucker or won't give with the seam or fabric. This is frequently the case with a loosely woven fabric, such as gauze. These selvages aren't suitable for reuse.

Selvages of bulky fabrics add too much thickness to seams.

If the selvage is wider than the pattern's seam allowance, don't use the selvage for seam finishing.

Some fabrics, such as linen-look suitings, have needle marks along the selvages, produced by the manufacturing process. Use these selvages only if they are going to be hidden.

Be careful when using selvages of sheer fabrics. If the selvage is darker or lighter in color, it may shadow-through the garment.

The edges of a knit fabric aren't termed "selvage." If you plan to use them, make certain the edges will give with the rest of the knit. On napped knits, be sure the nap continues into the edge and do not apply permanent stiffeners.

Uses for selvages

Seam finishing: Use the selvage as a self-finish on seams cut on the straight-of-grain in lightweight fabrics. Excellent candidates for this finish include the center back seam of straight-cut jackets or skirts and the center back slit of straight skirts.

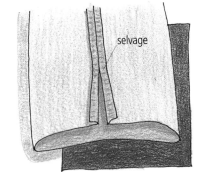

selvage

Back-slit skirt

Hemming: Plan the hem length for the lining in a straight skirt. Cut the lining on the crosswise grain, with the selvage creating the lower edge finish. The planning actually saves time because it reduces hemming, and the stronger lengthwise yarns positioned around the body take the strain through the hips, stomach, and thighs.

Eliminate bulk in the hem of straight-cut, pleated skirt styles by planning the hem length. Adjust the pattern, trimming excess length; cut the skirt on the crossgrain, positioning the pattern lower edge at the selvage edge.

To use selvage that differs noticeably in texture or color from the remainder of the fabric, place the pattern edge just above the inner selvage edge where the variation occurs. To hem, turn the selvage to the inside and machine-stitch.

> ✉ **Note:** This technique is also effective for hems on border prints with designs that run all the way along the selvage edge. Cut ruffles with one edge on the selvage to avoid tedious hemming.

Waistbands and cuffs: Cut waistbands and cuffs with one long edge on the selvage to eliminate a bulky seam allowance when turning the cuff or band to the wrong side.

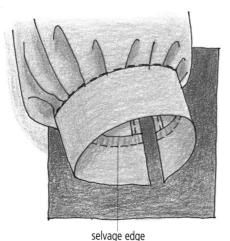

selvage edge

Sleeve cuff

Continuous plackets: Lay out a continuous placket for a sleeve or neck opening with one seamline on the selvage. Stitch the raw edge to the placket opening, fold the strip over the seam, and stitch it in place. This reduces bulk and also eliminates turning under a narrow hem.

Facings: Cut back or front yoke facings with the lower edge on the selvage, and stitch in-the-ditch to attach them to the completed garment.

Dirndl skirts: Cut simple dirndl skirts with the casing turnback edge on the selvage for a smooth and speedy finish.

Alternative to stay tape: Because selvages are so strong, they're the perfect replacement for stay tape on enclosed seams, such as those on V-necks or those on sheer fabrics requiring an exact match.

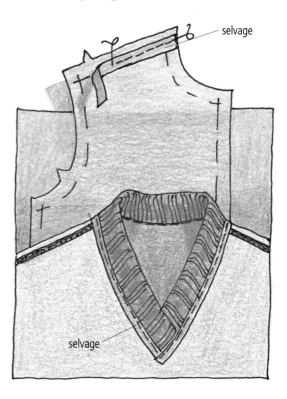

selvage

selvage

Selvage stay tapes

Slit tricks

To keep a skirt lining from showing at a slit or kick pleat, cut the lining lower edge in a curve at the opening edges.

Curved lining slit

To reinforce a skirt slit, sew a straight metal eye from a hook-and-eye closure at the slit upper point on the garment wrong side.

Straight eye reinforcement

Points perfect

Stitching professional-looking corners, collar points, and notched lapels on bulky fabrics can be a problem. But if you use a few simple tailoring techniques, every one of your corners and points will turn out perfectly. A little extra time during construction saves time correcting imperfections later.

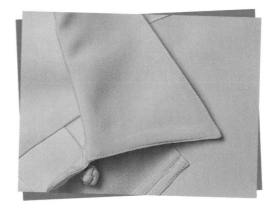

1. Before cutting your collar, redraw the sharp collar points, rounding them slightly. This step eliminates guessing when to take a stitch across the corner during construction.

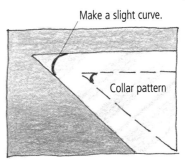

Make a slight curve.

Collar pattern

Redraw collar point.

2. Mark the stitching lines for undercollar points with a water-soluble pen.

3. With right sides together, baste the upper collar and undercollar together using short, even basting stitches.

4. Stitch the collar seam, adjusting the stitch length so that it is shorter than on other seams.

5. Remove the basting and press the seams flat. Next, press the seams open using a point presser.

6. To eliminate any ridges that might show through on the garment outside, grade the seam allowances. Trim the upper collar seam allowances to a little more than ¼", the undercollar seam allowances to a little less than ¼".

Trim the point of the seam allowances to ¹⁄₁₆" for tightly woven fabrics and to ⅛" for loosely woven fabrics, trimming at an angle.

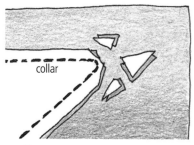

Trim seam allowances.

7. Fold the seam allowances in place against the upper collar wrong side, matching raw edges. Catchstitch the seam allowance edges flat against the collar. Repeat for the undercollar.

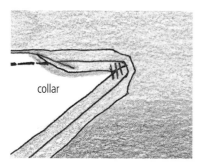

Catchstitch seam allowances.

8. Place the collar point on a point turner with the lengthwise seam allowance resting on top of the point turner. Hold the collar firmly and pull it over the end of the point turner, turning the collar right side out. Use the point turner as needed to straighten the collar points.

9. Cover a cutting board with a fabric scrap, right side up. Carefully position the collar, wrong side up, on the pressing surface so the edges are exactly where you want them. Cover the collar with a press cloth and press the edges with a steam iron, pounding the collar several times with a clapper to flatten the bulky edges.

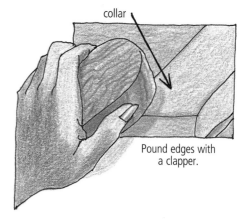

Flatten edges.

Three-in-one facing

Combining steps in garment construction is a great timesaver. This popular designer finish combines three techniques: interfacing with self-fabric, facing the garment edge, and finishing the facing raw edge. When used on straight edges at the front or back of garments that button, it's also the perfect solution for finishes that could show through lightweight fabric.

1. Trim away any existing facing at the front or back foldline edge; to that foldline add 1⅝" for the facing and 1½" for the self-fabric interfacing.

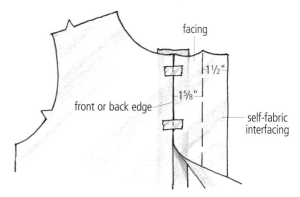

Trim at foldline.

2. Press the self-fabric interfacing allowance and then the facing allowance to the garment wrong side.

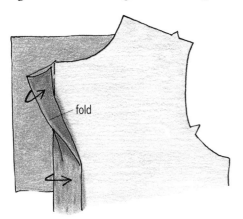

Press.

3. From the garment right side, topstitch 1/4" from the folded edge, catching the self-fabric interfacing raw edge in the stitching.

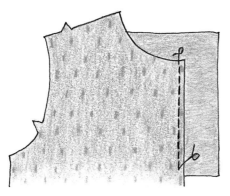

Topstitch.

4. Finish the neckline according to the pattern instructions.

Pinking power

Because serging has become the preferred seam-finishing technique, many sewers have relegated the pinking shears to the back of the sewing drawer. But you can put your pinking shears back to work to save you precious sewing time.

Pinking helps soften seam allowance edges and doesn't add the thread bulk created by serging. Use pinking shears for seam finishing when a seam allowance ridge may show on the garment outside after pressing.

Pink the outside edge of interfacing pieces before fusing them to the garment; there's less chance of show-through at the drop-off edge.

Notch and clip seam allowances (such as an outer collar edge) in one step with your pinking shears—one cut does both layers.

Decoratively pink edges as a simple finish for faux suedes and other nonraveling fabrics.

Reverse sewing

Stitching mistakes are never fun, but you can make the ripping process quicker (and safer) with the following handy tips:

- Always use sharp, narrow, pointed scissors or a seam ripper; dull tools can lead to irreversible mistakes.
- Clip a single stitch every inch along the seamline, and then carefully pick out the remaining stitches.
- On dark fabrics, rub light-colored chalk over the faulty stitching line to make the stitches easier for you to see.
- To keep slippery fabrics in place, first restitch the seam properly; then rip out the incorrect line.

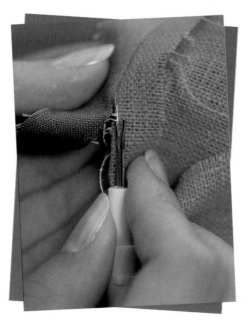

Give yourself a hand

If you need an extra hand to hold fabric while you "reverse-sew" a seam, use your sewing machine's presser foot. Simply place one end of the missewn seam under the presser foot and lower the foot—both hands will be free to "unsew" the seam for a faster fix.

Work with proper lighting, particularly when ripping out stitches on dark fabrics or when working late in the evening.

Pad news

You can camouflage a great number of figure imperfections by using shoulder pads in garments. In most garments the pads are invisible. But unfortunately, raglan-sleeved garments don't fall into this category. This unobstructed style of sleeve shows every stitch—whether it's tacked or attached with hoop-and-loop fasteners. But inserting a partial sleeve lining will let you pad raglan-sleeved shoulders without telltale signs. Here's how:

1. Purchase ¼ yard of lightweight woven or knit fabric for sleeve lining in a color that won't be visible from the garment right side. (Be sure the lining care instructions are compatible with the garment fabric.)

2. Pin the sleeve pattern to the front and back body pattern pieces. Hold the pattern pieces in place on your body and draw a line from the top of the sleeve pattern to the end of your shoulder.

3. Unpin the pattern pieces. On the sleeve pattern extend the shoulder line ½". Draw a second line across the pattern perpendicular to the shoulder line.

4. Trace the top of the sleeve pattern to make a lining pattern. Cut two linings from the sleeve lining fabric.

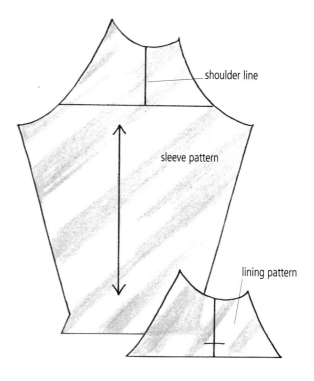

Draft sleeve-lining pattern.

Transfer the shoulder line and end of the shoulder markings to the sleeve linings.

5. Serge or overcast each lining's lower edge.

Finish lower edge.

6. Stitch the loop side of a hook-and-loop strip onto the right side of each sleeve lining, following the shoulder line. Stop at the end of the shoulder.

7. With wrong sides together, machine-baste the lining to the sleeve along the sides and top edge only, matching seamlines and neck edges. Don't stitch the lower finished edge of the lining to the sleeve.

Attach lining to sleeve.

8. Complete the garment according to the pattern instructions, and then attach sewn or purchased shoulder pads with hook-and-loop tape.

Shoulder savvy

Subtle shaping and soft support are key factors in sewing professional-looking sleeve caps. Use sleeve headers in garments with natural or slightly extended armholes to add extra pouf to full sleeves or a soft, rolled appearance to more tailored sleeves.

To make a sleeve header, cut a 3"x8" bias strip from lambswool, polyester fleece, or heavy cotton flannel. Make a 1" fold along one long side of the strip.

Matching centers, pin the folded edge of the strip to the wrong side of the sleeve. Overlap the armhole seam allowance ⅛". Slipstitch the folded edge to the seam allowance.

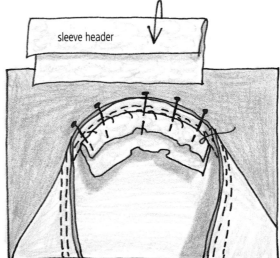

sleeve header

Position sleeve header.

If your garment has shoulder pads, stitch them in place as the pattern instructions indicate, extending them just slightly into the armhole.

All your shaping secrets will be covered by lining, giving your garment a professional look both inside and out!

Sleeve ease

Save time inserting set-in sleeves by following this unconventional method, which uses common rubber erasers! You'll need two standard firm erasers, approximately 1"x2".

> ✉ **Note:** Do not use white gum or art erasers, which may break or crumble.

Cut out and construct the garment up to and including sewing the shoulder seams, but leave the underarm seams open.

1. With right sides together, pin the sleeve cap to the garment armhole at each circle and notch, positioning the pins within the garment and not in the seam allowance, which should stay free of pins.

> ✉ **Note:** This process does not allow for a free hand to remove the pins as you sew!

2. Place the pinned sleeve/armhole under the presser foot with the sleeve wrong side up. Stitch to the first notch, using the required seam allowance.

3. Grasp an eraser lengthwise in each hand and firmly grip both fabric layers along the unsewn seamline just in front of the presser foot; the erasers will automatically ease away any excess fabric from the seamline.

4. Keeping a firm grip on the erasers, sew approximately the length of the erasers, making sure the sleeve cap fullness isn't puckering on the seamline. If puckers begin to form, simply lift the erasers and

Set-in sleeve

reposition them, gently easing the sleeve cap fullness outside the erasers.

5. Continue to stitch in the same manner, stopping every 1" to 2" to move the erasers forward, again checking for puckering. Repeat this procedure until you reach the second notch.

6. Set the erasers aside, complete the sleeve seam, and press it from the wrong side.

Four-way dressing

One garment worn four ways—it's the ultimate timesaver! Think of the potential for packing lightly.

Choose a sleeveless, scoopneck shell pattern with a dartless one-piece front and back and similarly cut front and back neckline.

Use four fabric colors—cut one front from each of two colors and one back from each of the remaining two colors.

Eliminate any facings in the pattern. With right sides facing, sew a front and back together. Repeat with the remaining front and back. With right sides facing, sew the two shells together, leaving an opening for turning. Turn through the opening and whipstitch the opening closed. Topstitch all edges (with matching thread colors) to prevent rolling.

Flip the blouse to suit your mood and your outfit.

color 1

color 2

color 3

color 4

Press test

As every fashion sewer knows, pressing as you sew is one of the keys to creating a beautiful garment. But all too often we're in a hurry and don't take the time to press even a basic seam correctly.

For perfect pressing every time:

• Select the correct iron temperature for your fabric.

• If the fabric can be steamed, let the steam do the work for you.

• Use a lift-and-lower motion.

• Use the proper pressing tools, such as a point presser, dressmaker's ham, or sleeve board.

After stitching the seam:

• Press it closed (the way it was sewn) to set the stitches and smooth the seam area.

Press seam flat, as stitched.

• To prevent impressions or ridges from showing on the fabric right side, press the seam over a seam roll.

• If the seam is curved, lay it over a dressmaker's ham and press.

• Allow the fabric to dry before handling.

• Pressing as you sew takes only a minute, and the results are well worth the effort.

• With the tip of the iron, press the seam allowances open, using your fingers to open the seam in front of the iron.

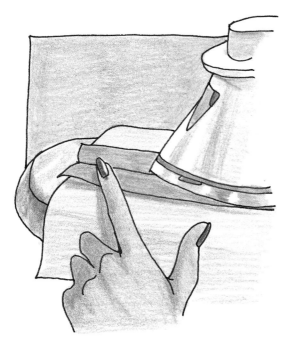

Press seam open.

Loop lingo

Enlist the help of your serger to make belt loops quickly and easily.

Triple belt loops

Cut a fabric strip that is long enough for all the belt loops and three times the finished width. Choose straight grain, or bias for a decorative look. Serge one long edge.

> ✉ **Note:** If you don't have a serger, use the fabric selvage for the finished edge.

Fold the strip lengthwise into thirds, with the serged edge on top. Topstitch close to both long edges. Cut the strip into individual belt loops.

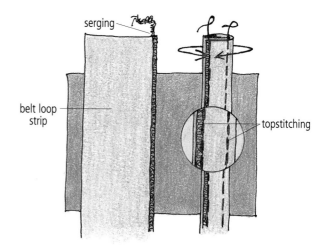

Triple-layer belt loops

Single-layer belt loops

If you don't need the stability of a multilayer belt loop, try the following:

Cut a fabric strip long enough for all the belt loops and ½" wider than the desired finished width. Serge both long strip edges.

Fold serged edges to the wrong side and topstitch in place. Depending on the belt loop width, you may be able to save time and topstitch both edges at once using a double needle.

Cut the strip into individual belt loops.

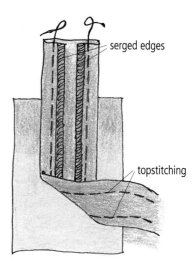

Single-layer belt loops

SINGLE-LAYER
CONSTRUCTION

Sewing a garment without interfacing, facings, or an undercollar sounds

like a challenge. But thanks to the countless choices of fabrics, suitable patterns, and

clever sewing techniques, single-layer construction can really save you time.

Pattern and fabric selection

Choose unstructured patterns (see box) for single-layer construction. They are easily adapted to single-layer construction, as are patterns with simple styling, clutch-style closures and few seams, darts, or other intricate details.

Good pattern choices

- Single- or double-breasted coats, ponchos, capes, and wrap coats
- Single- or double-breasted jackets with notched, shawl, or stand-up collars
- Garments with patch pockets
- Tops featuring kimono, raglan, dropped, or set-in sleeves without gathers or pleating

Choose a fabric with enough body to maintain its shape without interfacing or facings. Stretchy fabrics may become distorted during single-layer construction, never to return to their original shape.

Remember that in single-layer construction the fabric wrong side will show in turned-back areas, such as cuffs, collars, or lapels. When choosing a fabric, make sure the fabric is presentable on both sides; you can use one side as contrast trim for the other.

✉ **Note:** While some fabrics really have no right or wrong side, for instruction purposes we will refer to a "wrong" side.

Seam finishes

By selecting two-faced seam methods and edge finishes, you can create a completely reversible garment for twice the fashion impact in half the time.

Flat-felled seams

This is the classic reversible seam finish for straight seams. Fold under upper seam allowance. Trim under seam allowance.

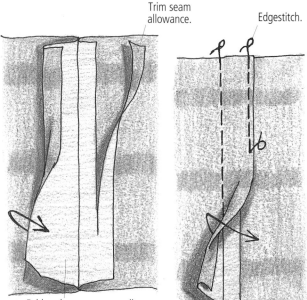

Trim seam allowance.

Edgestitch.

Fold under upper seam allowance.

Flat-felled seam

Edgestitched or clean-finished seams

These seams look like a trim because both fabric faces are exposed on the same side. This seam finish is best for light- to medium-weight fabrics. Fold under raw edges; topstitch.

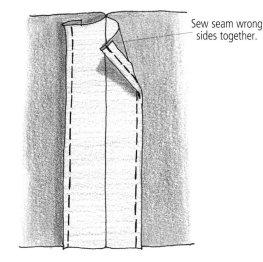

Sew seam wrong sides together.

Edgestitched seam

Taped seams

Use taped seams, in which braid or single-fold bias binding covers the raw edges, on any shape of seam.

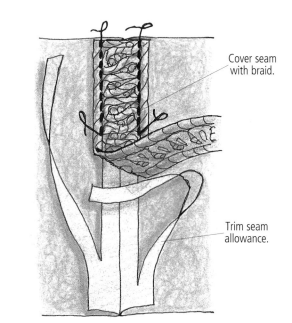

Cover seam with braid.

Trim seam allowance.

Taped seam

Bound seams

Bound seams are suitable for inside or outside the garment. They're particularly attractive when coordinated with a binding on the outside edges.

Bound seam

Decorative lapped seams

Form a lapped seam by laying a decoratively finished seam allowance over the top of a seam allowance that has been regularly finished. Match the ⅝" stitching lines, and then topstitch into place. Lapped seams require advance planning—the pattern must fit, as there's no room for altering, and you must decide before stitching which seam allowance will be exposed and which will be on the inside of the garment.

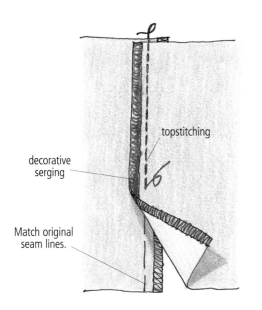

Decorative serged lapped seam

On the edge

Finish reversible garment edges using one of the following methods:

Pulled fringe

To fringe, first establish the fringe depth with a line of staystitching. Pull away the threads below the staystitching to form the fringe.

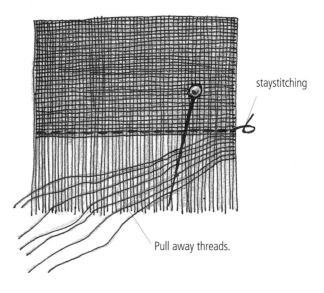

Pulled-thread fringe

Ravel fringe

Snip in ½" to ¾"-wide strips. On knits such as fleece, the snipped edges will roll to the right side; on fabrics such as denim, the edges will fray softly when washed and dried.

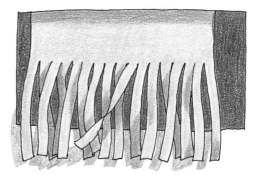

Ravel fringe

Binding

Bind the garment edge with purchased bias trim, or make your own bias binding from a contrasting fabric.

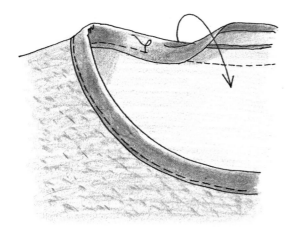

Binding from contrasting fabric

Serging

Serge the raw edge of firm, stable fabrics with a wide, balanced, or 2- or 3-thread stitch using decorative thread, or adjust tensions to create a blanket-stitch look. Pearl cotton, crochet thread, lightweight yarns, and texturized nylon thread are all suitable for decorative edge finishes and lapped seams. Novelty threads will make lapel, hem, and pocket edges look like they are braid trimmed.

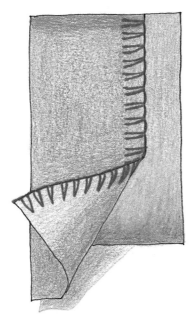

Serged blanket stitch

Serging with heavy decorative threads

1. Begin with a stitch length that is longer than usual (3.5mm to 4mm).
2. Use heavy thread in the loopers only and a matching all-purpose thread in the needle.
3. Loosen the looper tensions. Fine-tune the length and tension settings, test-stitching on scraps until you get the desired stitch appearance.
4. Keep some slack in the novelty thread between the spool and the machine.
5. Sew slowly.

✎ **Note:** Curved and bias edges can stretch regardless of fabric weight, so staystitch the garment edges using a conventional sewing machine. Stitch $\frac{1}{2}$" from the cut edge on all pieces. The decorative edge at the seamline will conceal the staystitching. If the edge needs more than staystitching for stability, serge over two strands of matching thread when you apply the edge finish.

Pockets

Add patch pockets to single-layer fabrics for a great look. To reinforce pockets, fuse interfacing to the wrong side and then serge along the seamline and facing edges with decorative thread, trimming away the seam allowance. Use a conventional sewing machine to straight stitch the pockets to the garment front on the placement lines.

Collars

With single-layer construction, attaching collars and finishing front openings can be done simultaneously.

Notched collars

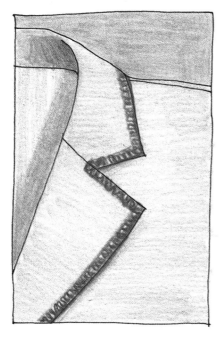

Omit the facing and interfacing; finish the collar outside raw edges. Using decorative thread in both loopers, sew the unfinished collar neckline edge to the garment as you finish the front opening raw edge.

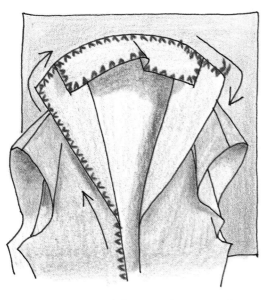

Notched collar: Stitch following direction of arrows.

On the jacket right side, begin serging the hem at one open side seam. Serge around the jacket outside in one step—hem, lapel, across the collar (removing pins well ahead of serging lapel). Hem, ending at the open side seam.

Lap the open side seam and topstitch it in place on a conventional sewing machine.

Press the decorative seam allowance toward the collar. If desired, topstitch through this decorative seam and the collar to hold it flat.

Shape the collar and lapels on the roll line and lightly steam.

> ✉ **Note:** This seam will be concealed by the collar roll.

Shawl collars

Omit the facing and interfacing. Finish the raw edges of the collar and front opening simultaneously.

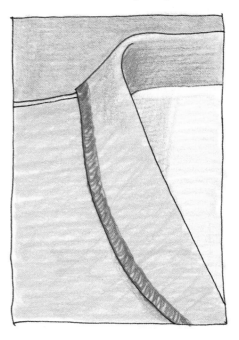

Shawl collar: Finish front opening edges as you stitch.

FAST FUSIBLES

In recent years, sewing technology

has advanced considerably. With the introduction

of fusibles, tasks that previously involved hours of hand

sewing can now be finished faster using

no-sew techniques.

FUSE NEWS

Like the serger, fusible products have changed the way we sew. With many sewing projects today, you'll spend as much time fusing at the ironing board as you will stitching at the sewing machine—and you'll finish faster.

Fusible products

Adhesives may be the most versatile fusible product on the market. You can find them in many forms—from semisheer web to solid glue.

Use fusibles products for . . .

- Bonding hems.
- Creating primary seams.
- Stabilizing garment areas.
- Attaching shoulder pads.
- Applying trims.
- Changing hand of fabric.

Fusible adhesives are available by the yard and in various precut strips, sized to match common ribbon, seam allowance, and hem widths. You'll find light, heavy, and super weights to work with many different fabrics and for a variety of tasks.

Many webs and glues come with a paper backing that acts as a protective press cloth so you can heat-baste the adhesive just where you want it before permanently bonding. The paper backing may be plain, gridded to help you measure strips and enlarge charted designs, or preprinted with popular appliqué shapes like hearts and stars. Most backings are transparent enough to allow you to trace patterns and designs directly onto them before applying the fusible to the fabric; you can then fuse decorative motifs cleanly and seal to the raw edge.

> **Note:** Don't forget to trace patterns in reverse, as you'll flop the design during permanent application.

You'll also find a wide selection of ready-made appliqués, mending patches, hook-and-loop tapes, and fashion trims with web already applied to the wrong side for easy, no-sew embellishing and quick repairs.

Liquid fusible

This form of heat-activated glue was developed for wearable artists and fabric crafters. Squeeze the creamy liquid directly onto the fabric and trims, or use a foam brush to spread it on the back of openwork materials such as lace. Once the web dries, fuse the treated fabric or trim permanently into position.

Iron-on stabilizer

Apply this nonwoven sheet to the fabric wrong side to stabilize it for decorative stitching or appliqué. Then tear away and discard the stabilizer when the project is complete.

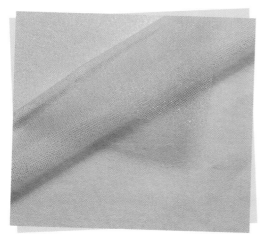

Fusible vinyl

Laminated to the fabric right side, this add-on creates a water- and stain-resistant finish that makes the fabric useful indoors and out. Choose either the matte or shiny vinyl for projects such as patio furniture cushions, picnic tablecloths, kitchen accessories, shower curtains, or aprons. Because the vinyl surface coating is washable and remains flexible after fusing, this product is also suitable for fashion-sewing items such as raincoats, umbrellas, and luggage.

Fusible fleece

Designed to eliminate pinning and basting, fusible fleece can be used in quilts, dimensional appliqués, placemats, and insulated garments. Simply cut the fleece to size and iron it lightly to the wrong side of one fabric layer. The adhesive prevents shifting as you stitch through the layers and maintains a uniformly padded surface.

Fusible tapes

Home-decorating enthusiasts can make quick work of sewing projects with fusible tapes. Use fusible tapes to form instant pleats and gathers for drapery headers, and fusible Roman shade tape for pull-up blinds.

Fusible interfacings

In most fabric stores, fusible interfacings outnumber sew-ins. No longer stiff like their predecessors, today's interfacings vary in weight from sheer to heavy-duty. For a secure, permanent bond, simply follow the manufacturer's instructions regarding heat, moisture, time, and pressure.

Fusible thread

Spun from all-nylon fibers or from polyester with a heat-sensitive nylon filament added, this thread provides an iron-on substitute for pinning and thread-basting. Wind it onto the bobbin; then, with all-purpose thread in the needle, stitch to create iron-in-place hems, bias bindings, decorative appliqués, zippers, and patch pockets. Use fusible thread in the lower looper of your serger for mock passementerie-braid trim and decorative edgings. Once you've used the iron to melt the filament, the basted detail is ready for permanent stitching.

Ironing melts the fusible element of the thread to form a bond with the fabric, making this thread perfect for fuse-basting. A portion of the thread remains firmly intact for permanent seaming.

On a conventional sewing machine, it's easiest to use fusible thread in the bobbin with a slightly loosened tension and all-purpose thread in the needle. To position the fusible on the fabric right side, simply stitch with the fabric wrong side up. On some conventional machines, fusible thread can also be used in the needle, though a size 14 or larger needle is required.

When sewing with a straight stitch, use a stitch length that is slightly longer than normal, approximately 8 to 10 stitches per inch (2.5mm to 3mm). For zigzagging, an average stitch (3mm wide and 2mm long) will suit most of your needs; thick or heavy fabrics will require a wider zigzag stitch. To adhere the thread, use your iron on a steam setting. Trim thread ends and place a press cloth on the fabric to avoid bonding the thread to your iron or ironing board.

On a serger, use fusible thread in the lower looper, adjusting tensions as needed for a balanced stitch.

Use fusible thread for . . .

Seam allowances. Finish raveling seam allowance edges on thick fabrics. Press seam open. Zigzag close to seam allowance edges; fuse.

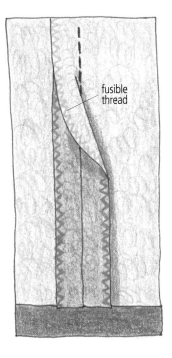

Seam finishing

Facings. Understitch facings to prevent rolling. Stitch close to seamline, catching seam allowances. Fold facing inside garment; fuse understitching.

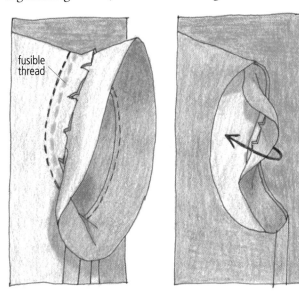

Facings

Buttons. Secure machine-sewn buttons—touch the iron point to fuse the underside of stitching.

Zippers. Hold zippers in place before topstitching. Fuse-baste zipper wrong side up over seamline.

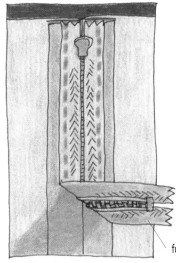

Zippers

Appliqués. Fuse-baste appliqués and trims in place before permanent stitching.

Appliqués

Hems. Finish hem edges on the fabric wrong side; press the hem in place.

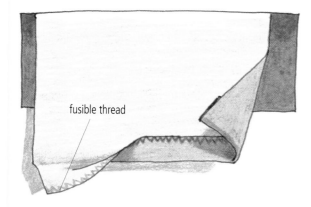

Hems

Lapped seams. Fuse-baste lapped seams before final stitching.

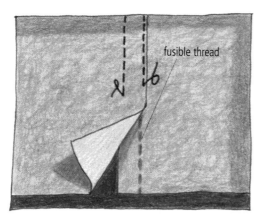

Lapped seams

Binding. Hold binding in position for stitching in-the-ditch.

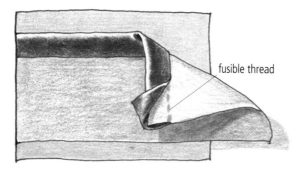

Binding

Pressing facts

To save your iron soleplate from frequent cleanings, be sure to use a press cloth when using fusible products. A lightweight broadcloth works well, but if visibility is important, choose a more see-through fabric such as organdy or organza for your press cloth.

For an environmentally sound option, recycle clean packing tissue or pull out your old patterns and use the pattern tissue as a press cloth. Tissue is inexpensive, transparent, and reusable, and it offers iron protection.

> ✉ **Note:** If using the pattern tissue for a press cloth, test it first on a fabric scrap to make sure the ink does not transfer to the fabric.

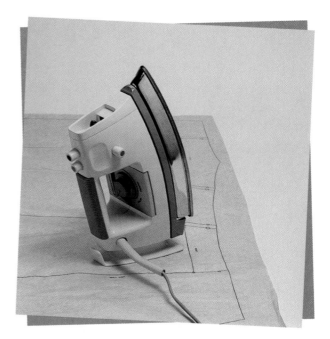

Great glue

If glue isn't in your sewing basket, you may be spending more time than necessary on some sewing projects. Glue has always been indispensable for crafts projects, but it's often overlooked by fashion-sewers.

There are three types of glues that are of interest to fashion-sewers. Each has different properties and uses. **Glue sticks** are adhesives in lipstick-like containers for easy, convenient application. Some are permanent, others only temporary; some dry clear, others white. Check the label before you glue.

White glues all share the same basic formula but vary in thickness and sticking strength; the thicker the glue, the less moisture it contains and the less it will soak through fabric. All white glues dry clear and are nontoxic and odorless. Some white glues will hold up through one or two washings, but they aren't permanent.

How to glue

You can sometimes use a glue stick and white glue interchangeably. Generally, however, glue stick is best for quick, temporary basting jobs and white glue, which has greater sticking strength, is better for more precise applications. Give the glue time to bond properly so that your glued piece will not shift while you stitch. And if the glue has fully bonded, there will be no danger of gumming up the needle.

Use a glue stick for . . .

- Basting.
- Positioning braid, ribbon, or other trims.
- Positioning pockets or zippers.
- Holding buttons in place.
- Holding lapped seams. Apply the glue to the turned-under edge and position the fold along the seamline for a perfect seam.
- Basting a seam when matching plaids. (If you'll be pressing the seam allowances open later, remember to apply the glue along the stitching line only, not all over the seam allowances.)
- Attaching underlining to a garment that requires two layers of fabric to be handled as one. Apply small dots or a thin line of glue along the seam edge away from the stitching line. Allow the glue to set before handling.

Permanent fabric glues, when fully bonded, can withstand machine washing and drying; on certain fabrics, a few can even be dry-cleaned.

If you need a glue that won't wash out, choose a permanent fabric adhesive. It forms a strong, permanent bond between fabrics and can replace thread in many instances. You can use this glue alone to hold an appliqué in place, or you can stitch over it when completely dry.

Use permanent fabric glue for . . .

- Mending and patching.
- Hemming.
- Attaching hook-and-loop strips or dots.
- Adhering zippers.
- Holding belt edges, pockets, or flat-felled seams.
- Applying bias tape.
- Attaching appliqués, beads, sequins, braids, and trims.

FUSIBLE SHORTCUTS

Fusibles may save more time for sewers than any other technological advance. Use them for hemming, matching plaids and stripes, and covering cording.

Piping power

Tired of guessing which line of stitching you should be following as you sew covered piping into a seam? Try this simplified method for making piping. You won't have to guess, since there won't be any stitching lines to hide.

Wrap the cord with fusible web and the bias fabric. Then press the raw fabric edges together. The result? Perfect piping with no stitching!

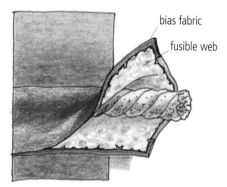

Covering cording

Knee notes

To extend the life of children's pants, reinforce the knee area of both legs with a patch of fusible knit interfacing. Use your pinking shears to cut a 4"x6" rectangle of interfacing for each leg, and then fuse one to each knee area wrong side.

When the knees of the pants eventually wear thin, cut the pant legs off to make shorts. Hem or cuff the leg lower edge.

Painless hems

If hand hemming isn't your thing, you can hem pants or skirts quickly by applying a narrow fusible web strip just inside the hem edge, following the manufacturer's instructions. To keep the web from creeping out of the hem as you press, serge it to the hem edge wrong side. You'll create a professionally finished hem edge and hold the web in place at the same time.

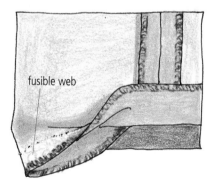

Hemming

A perfect match

Plaids add an exciting dimension to fashion, and matching the plaid's design results in a professional-looking garment that is fun to wear. Use fusibles and follow this timesaving technique to keep your plaid lines matched.

Plaids should flow around the body, matching at the side seams, center front, center back, and front armhole notch. The design should also maintain a continuous vertical line from the top of the garment to the bottom.

When cutting out a plaid, first position the most important pattern piece—the front of the garment. Always match stitching lines, not cutting lines.

Once pattern pieces are properly cut, use this fusible basting tape technique to create perfectly matched seams every time, even with plaids cut on the bias!

Steps to a perfect plaid match
1. Press under the seam allowance on one garment section.
2. Place basting tape ⅟₁₆" from the seam allowance fold on the pressed-under portion. Peel away the paper backing from the basting tape.
3. Position the folded seam allowance on top of the corresponding garment section, matching the design at the seamline.

4. From the wrong side of the garment, stitch the seam using the folded creaseline as a guide.
5. Remove the basting tape before pressing.

Don't make waves!

If you like narrow, topstitched hems but not the ripples and waves that often appear on hems of flared or circular skirts, calm the waves with interfacing! Use a ¾"-wide strip of lightweight fusible tricot interfacing cut on the bias to conform to the curve of the hem and give with the fabric. This simple technique will also add body and improve the drape and hang of the hem.

How to create a ripple-free hem
1. Mark the hem foldline.
2. Trim the hem allowance to 1".
3. Position the interfacing on the wrong side of the hem allowance with the interfacing lower edge even with the hem foldline. Fuse according to the manufacturer's instructions.
4. Finish the hem raw edge.
5. Fold the hem allowance to the wrong side along the hem foldline; pin at right angles to the fold.
6. On the fabric right side, topstitch ⅝" from the folded edge.

basting tape

Matching plaids

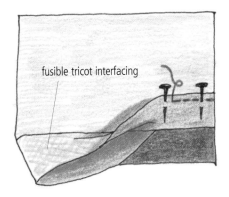

fusible tricot interfacing

Ripple-free hem

MACHINE
MAGIC

Little did our grandmothers suspect that their treadle machines would become antique collectibles, replaced by computerized sewing machines and sergers. Tasks like buttonholes and finished seams that took them hours to complete by hand now take half the time.

THE SERGER MERGER

Sergers, long a secret of the ready-to-wear industry,

can save you time and help you add a professional look to the garments you create.

Most commercial patterns don't include serging instructions,

but don't let that stop you. Here's how to use this machine to your best advantage.

Serger shortcuts

When sewing garments exclusively on a serger, remember that a stitch in time saves nine. Reinforce heavy stress areas, such as crotch seams, with conventional straight stitching. Here are some other serging tips to keep in mind:

Seaming

Before serging any garment seams, you *must* be sure the pattern fits you, as seam allowances are trimmed away during the serging process.

Ravel prevention

One of the best ways to prevent seams from raveling is to serge around all fabric pieces before beginning construction.

Serged fabric edges

In-seam pockets

When creating an in-seam pocket, serge each pocket piece to its respective garment panel, trimming the excess seam allowances. Then press each seam allowance toward the pocket.

Waistbands

Serge-finish the unnotched edge of a waistband to eliminate the bulk of a turned-under finish. Then serge-finish the waistband underlap end for a flat finish.

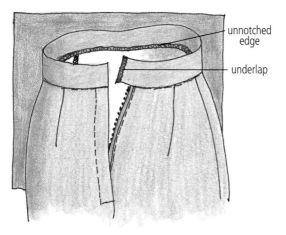

Serged waistband edges

Hemming

Serge-finish the raw edge of the hem. Pin the hem in place, and then stitch by hand or use a machine to blindhem or a twin needle to topstitch.

Blindhemming

Press under the hem allowance and baste it ¼" from the raw edge. Adjust the serger for 2- or 3-thread flatlocking, and attach the serger's blindhem foot. Fold the hem onto the garment right side at the basting line; position the hem under the serger foot so

the needle barely catches the fold and the knives trim just a hint of the excess hem allowance *without* cutting the fold.

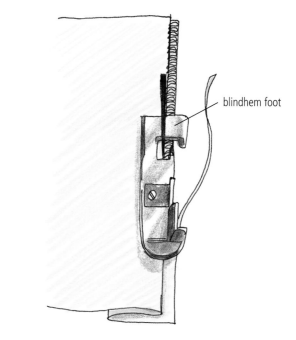

Serged blindhem

Open the completed hem, and press. "Ladders" will appear on the garment right side, and the raw edge on the wrong side will be serge finished.

> ✉ **Note:** Using the serger for blindhemming lets you finish the raw edge and hem the garment at the same time.

Rolled hems

The rolled hem is an especially decorative and practical serger option that you can incorporate easily into conventional patterns. Use these narrow, beautifully finished hems on lightweight fabrics and evening attire, as well as on ruffle edges on everything from feminine blouses to little girls' dresses.

Facings

Serge-finish the front facing raw edge. On less stable fabrics, straight stitch ⅜" from the garment edge before serging the facing to the garment.

In many cases, a serger allows you to omit neckline and armhole facings and hems on garments made of stable fabrics. An edge serged with a decorative thread does the trick in one easy step.

Sheers

In garments made from sheer fabrics, serge narrow seams. The seams will disappear.

Elastic casings

> ✉ **Note:** This technique permits you to finish the casing raw edge and create a casing simultaneously.

Press a 1" to 1½" casing to the inside along the garment upper edge. Fold the casing back onto the garment right side so the casing raw edge is even with the new fold. Serge with your blindhem foot, trimming a scant ¹⁄₁₆" from the casing raw edge only—do not cut the garment fold. Allow the needle to barely nip the fold. Leave an opening for inserting the elastic; after inserting, topstitch the opening closed.

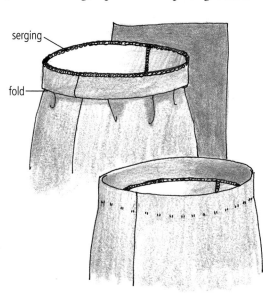

serging

fold

Serged casing

Decorative edges

Using novelty threads in serger loopers can create a host of decorative edge finishes and flatlocked seaming options. Check your machine instruction manual for details.

Topstitching

Sergers with chainstitch and coverstitch options do not require you to stay close to the fabric edge as conventional sergers do, so you can use them for topstitching within a garment.

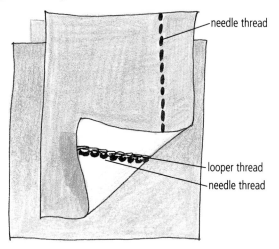

needle thread

looper thread
needle thread

Chainstitching

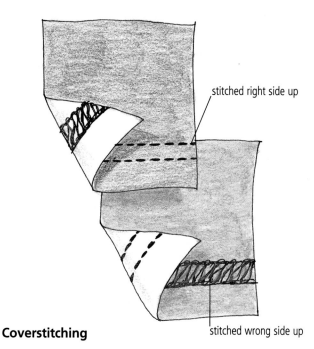

stitched right side up

stitched wrong side up

Coverstitching

Distinctly differential

Taking advantage of your serger's differential feed capability can speed your sewing time and revolutionize how you perform certain sewing tasks.

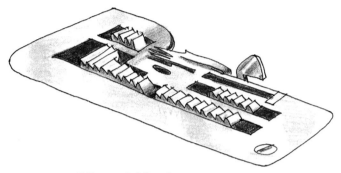

Serger differential feed

Serger feed dogs, the metal teeth that protrude through the throat plate, work in tandem with the presser foot to grip the fabric and move it along during sewing. Sergers equipped with differential feed have two sets of feed dogs, one in front and one in back, each capable of working at different rates. The normal setting may be labeled "N" or "1", which means the feed dogs move at a 1-to-1 ratio—the same rate.

If the adjustable dial is set on 2, the front feed dogs take in twice as much fabric under the presser foot as the rear feed dogs release. The effect is similar to that of "ease-plussing" on a conventional machine (placing your finger behind the presser foot to restrict feeding), which causes the fabric to draw up into slight puckers or gathers.

The differential feed dial can also be set below normal. The minimum on most sergers is 0.7, but a few can go as low as 0.5. With these settings, the front feed dogs take in a fraction (seven-tenths or one-half) as much fabric under the foot as the rear feed dogs release. "Taut sewing" (holding the fabric taut in front and in back of the presser foot) produces the same results, but why not let your serger do the work?

The amount of stretching or gathering will vary depending on the differential feed setting, the stitch length, and the fabric weight.

Above-normal or plus settings

• Serge stretchy fabrics (sweatering, bias edges) to offset rippling.
• Ease or gather nonstretchy fabrics—hem a flared skirt.

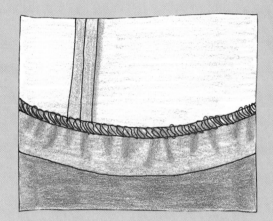

• Make yards of gathered ruffles for home-decorating projects.

Below-normal or minus settings

• Create a smooth seam and pucker-free rolled edges on lightweight fabrics.
• Add a rippled lettuce-hem edge.

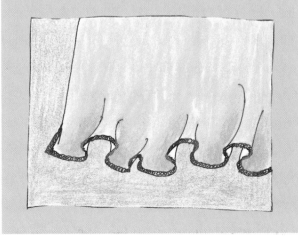

CONVENTIONAL STITCHES

No matter how wonderful a serger is, sometimes design, fit, seam strength,

or ease of handling during construction makes the basic stitches of a conventional

sewing machine hard to beat.

Basic techniques

The stitches of your conventional machine can't be beat when it comes to these basic tailoring techniques.

Jackets

A serged seam cannot be trimmed and graded, and serging is difficult to maneuver in tight corners. A conventional machine works best for jacket lapels, where grading is needed to reduce bulk in the pressed seam and notched areas.

Collars

Prepare a two- or four-piece collar on a conventional machine so that you can grade inside seams and stitch and trim collar points accurately.

Topstitching

For even, flat topstitching, straight stitch the seams involved and grade the seam allowances. A serged seam is generally too bulky under topstitching and will result in uneven spacing and stitch length when you use more than one row of topstitching.

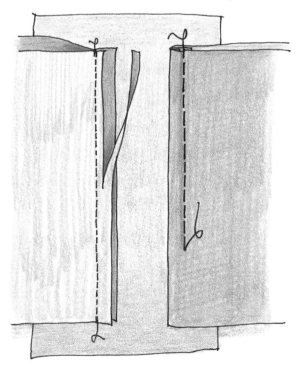

Trimming seams

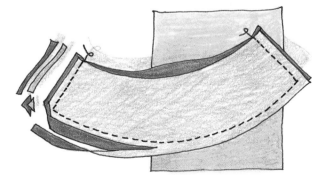

Grading seams

Necklines

Because the inside angles at the corners of square, faced necklines require clipping close to the stitching, serging is not ideal. Conventional straight stitching is a must for the corner to turn properly.

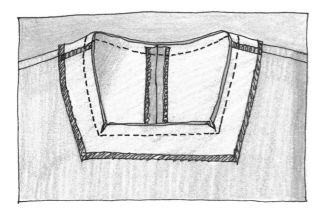

Clipping corners

Ribbing

Although it's easy to serge ribbing to a garment, you should use a conventional sewing machine to stitch the ribbing band in a circle to reduce bulk in the seamline. Straight stitch the ribbing ends, and then finger-press the seam allowance open.

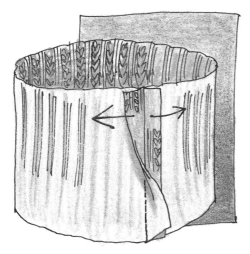

Straight stitching ribbing ends

Elastic

Joining elastic ends with a serged seam creates a very bulky area. Lap elastic ends and straight stitch or zigzag in a square pattern instead.

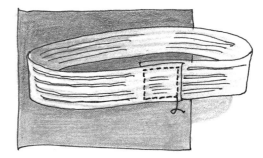

Joining elastic ends

Sleeves

Although you can set in sleeves using the serger, most fabrics require two easestitching lines for even distribution of fullness. Use your conventional machine for stitching a fitted sleeve and then you can serge-finish the sleeve seam allowance.

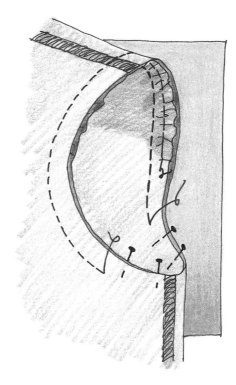

Stitching a set-in sleeve

Piping and welting

The width of a standard serger presser foot prevents serging close to the edge of piping and welting. It's generally better to use a conventional machine and a zipper foot to sew these trims snugly into a seam. Some sergers, however, do feature a cording or piping foot, allowing for close-up serging.

Darts

You can sew darts with a serger, but the serger knives cut away the folded portion of the dart, making adjustments impossible. Controlling the serger stitching at the dart point is extremely difficult. Choose conventional straight stitching for the best-looking (and adjustable) results.

Two-for-one topstitching

Why waste time stitching twice when you can stitch two rows in one pass? Twin-needle topstitching produces two rows of stitching at once. It's great for hems because it's secure and also creates a subtle decorative effect. Also use it for topstitching facings and elastic and for attaching pockets. To get started, all you need is a sewing machine that zigzags and a twin needle.

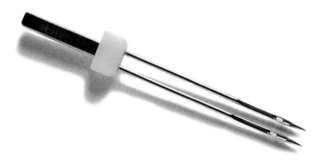

Twin needles range in size from 1.6mm/size 70 to 6.0mm/size 100. The first number is the distance between the needles; the second is the size of the needles. A 2.0mm/size 80 is a good general-purpose twin needle.

For twin-needle stitching:

1. Use two spools of thread. Follow the normal threading path with both threads.

2. At the tension disk, place one thread on the left side of the disk and the other on the right.

3. At the last thread guide (just above the needle), place one thread in the left guide, one thread in the right. If your machine has only one guide, put one thread in and leave the other out.

4. Set your machine for straight stitching, and turn the hand wheel to lower the needles slowly, checking that they don't hit the throat plate or presser foot.

5. If skipped stitches occur, move the needle position slightly to the left.

6. For a raised pin-tuck effect, tighten both the top and bobbin thread tensions.

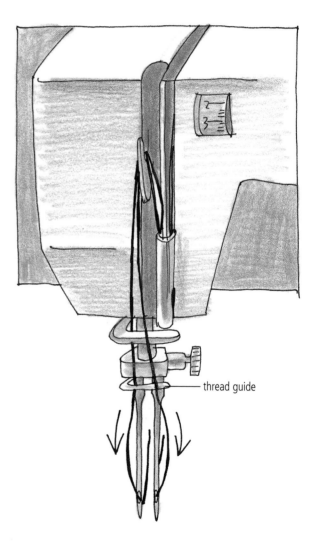

thread guide

Threading a twin needle

Double take

Tired of topstitching disappearing into your jacket lapel? Try this easy technique to make your stitching stand out:

1. Use two strands of thread through a single needle. On textured fabrics, choose two colors for a custom-blended look.

2. Separate the thread strands at the tension disks and thread guides, and then join them before threading the needle.

3. If your machine isn't equipped with two spool pins, wind a bobbin of the second color and place it under the spool. Or extend a single spool pin by placing a drinking straw over the shaft to make room for the second spool.

4. Test-stitch on a sample that has the same number of layers as your garment; adjust tensions and stitch length. If the thread breaks or shreds, choose a needle in a larger size.

Don't limit this pairing technique to topstitching. Double-thread buttonholes are firmer and hold their shape better than single-strand buttonholes—no cording needed.

Getting edgy

Always popular on expensive ready-to-wear clothing, decorative hems, bindings, pipings, and fringes are a cinch to duplicate.

Topstitched hems

These simple hems work on everything from sportswear to eveningwear.

1. Cut the garment with an additional 1⅝" to 2¼" hem allowance, depending on the flare of the skirt.

2. Steam-press the hem allowance to the wrong side and shrink out any fullness. Finish raw edges.

3. Topstitch with matching or contrasting thread, all-purpose or buttonhole twist, close to the foldline and then ¼" away.

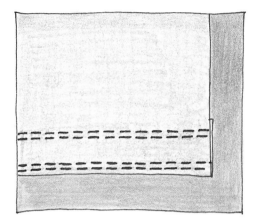

Topstitched hem

4. Depending on the hem allowance width, leave a ¾" to 1¼" space (the wider the hem, the wider the spacing) and topstitch again. If desired, topstitch one more time ¼" from the previous stitching, close to the garment's turned-under edge.

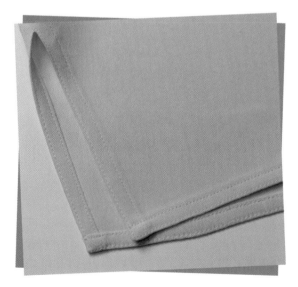

Narrow topstitched hem

Pinked or scalloped edges

Another finish, particularly attractive on denim or suede, is a simple pinked or scalloped edge. Don't worry about fraying on wovens—that's part of the charm.

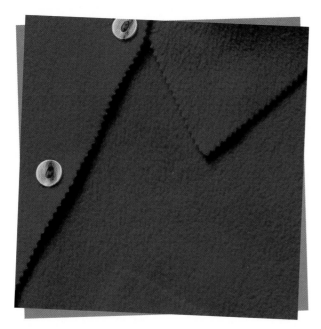

Zigzag finishes

Cut off the hem allowance. Zigzag (wide width, medium length) over the raw edge, stitching with the grain to minimize fraying. To produce a flatter edge, use an overcast foot or apply a water-soluble stabilizer under the hem edge.

For a prettier finish when stitching over a hem edge, allow the needle to stitch off the fabric as it swings to the right.

Lettuce ripples

This ripple technique works best on fabrics with at least 50% stretch. Avoid single knits that may run when stretched.

1. Cut the garment with a ⅝" hem allowance.

2. With the hem folded under and stretched as much as possible, zigzag (medium width, short length) over the folded edge.

3. Trim excess hem allowance close to the stitches.

Lettuce hem

Shell hemming

Use a blindhem stitch to make a shell hem.

1. Cut the garment with a ⅝" hem allowance and fold the hem to the wrong side.

2. Position the garment under the presser foot with the bulk of the fabric toward the right, under the arm of the sewing machine.

> ✉ **Note:** If your machine has mirror imaging, you can use that feature and place the fabric with the bulk toward the left.

3. Tighten the tensions and set the machine for a blindhem stitch. Although you can vary the stitch length and width, a medium setting makes an attractive small scallop.

4. Stitch the hem in place, allowing the "bite" of the blind hem to go off the folded edge.

5. Trim away excess hem allowance.

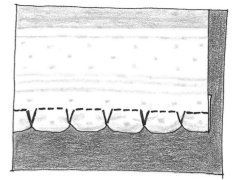

Shell hem

Satin-stitched edges

You can use a simple satin stitch to simulate a serger-rolled hem. For a smooth finish, use machine embroidery thread and an appliqué foot.

1. Cut the garment with a ⅝" hem allowance, and fold the hem under.

2. Zigzag (narrow width, medium length) over the folded edge.

3. Trim excess seam allowance, and satin stitch (medium width, short length) the edge.

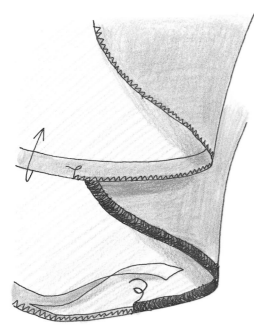

Satin-stitched hem

The edge will roll more easily if you use a buttonhole foot. Experiment with the fabric right side up and right side down to get the smoothest finish on your particular machine.

Once you've mastered the rolled edge, finish the edges of patch pockets, bands, and collars before stitching them in place.

Pipings

Although it's usually corded and bias cut, piping can also be flat and straight grain, depending on the application. Either way, it's easier to apply if it's shaped to fit the garment edge before being stitched.

Purchased piping

To apply purchased piping:

1. Cut the garment seam allowances to ⅜".

2. Stitch the piping to the garment right side.

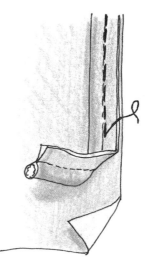

Applying purchased piping

3. Secure the piping between the garment and strip of fabric. Fold the fabric strip under, and press.

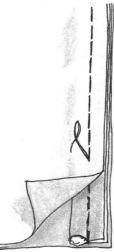
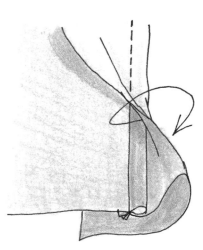

Finishing purchased piping

Custom piping

To create piping with your own fabric:

1. Fold the fabric strip in half lengthwise, wrong sides together. If the piping is to be corded, wrap the strip around the cord.

2. Machine-stitch the desired distance (the finished width of the piping) from the folded edge, and trim the seam allowances to the desired width. If the piping is corded, stitch using a zipper foot.

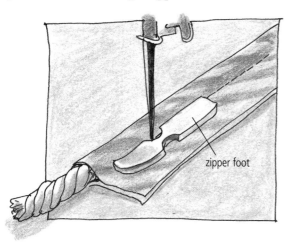

zipper foot

Covering cord

3. To make multiple cords, stitch piping over piping until the trim is the desired width. Use pipings of different colors for a creative look.

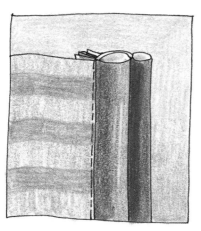

Multiple cords

> ✉ **Note:** Sandwich pipings between the garment and a facing or lining for a neater inside finish.

Scalloped elegance

Because corded scallops look like hand-crocheted lace, they add an elegant touch to collars, cuffs, tucks, and hems. The cording is necessary since you'll be sewing off the fabric edge. Use size 8 pearl cotton, and stitch on paper or stabilizer that you will tear away later. Here's how to make corded scallops:

1. Set the machine for a scalloped satin stitch (refer to your sewing machine manual for length, width, and needle position settings).

2. Use an embroidery presser foot, and tighten the bobbin tension.

3. Place the paper or stabilizer under the fabric so that it extends 1" past the edge. Position the fabric edge so that only the point of the scallop catches the fabric.

4. Hold the cord loosely in your right hand while guiding the fabric with your left hand.

5. When the stitching is complete, carefully tear the paper or stabilizer away.

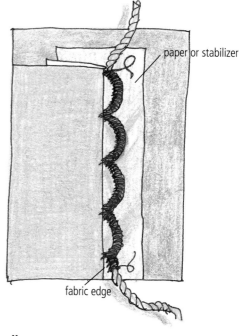

paper or stabilizer

fabric edge

Corded scallops

Place that lace

Lace, one of the most elegant and feminine finishes for almost any edge, is easily attached using the zigzag stitch on your sewing machine.

Two-step application (for knits):

1. Lay the straight edge of the lace along the right side of the seamline and stitch it in place with a fairly close, medium-width zigzag.

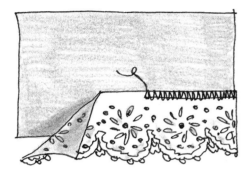

2. From the reverse side, trim the fabric close to the stitching.

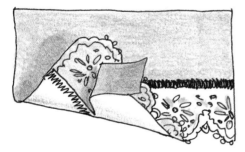

Three-step application (for woven fabrics):

1. Position and stitch the lace as described in the two-step application, but use a widely spaced zigzag.

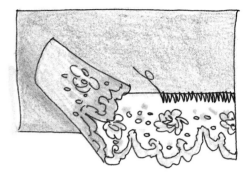

2. Fold the fabric edge back against the zigzagging and stitch again from the right side, using a slightly wider and denser zigzag.

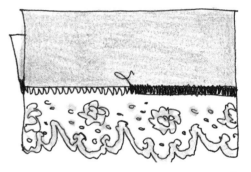

3. Trim the fabric close to the stitching line.

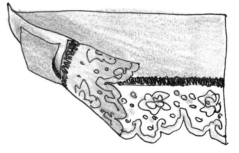

YARNS, THREADS, AND NEEDLES

Using novelty yarns in your serger can be a challenge. The key to perfect stitches is an even yarn tension, but achieving perfection is easier said than done.

Pull-ups

You can enlist a friend's help to pull slack yarn from the skein so your serger doesn't "blip." Or, if you're sewing alone, you must stop and pull enough slack to continue sewing for a distance, and then repeat the process. Both methods are time consuming.

To make a nontangling yarn ball that pulls from the center, follow these steps:

1. Snap the loose yarn end under the cap on a plastic pill bottle.

2. Wind the skeined yarn around the bottle below the cap line until you have the amount needed for your project.

3. Release the capped yarn end and pull out the bottle. The newly freed yarn end should pull without a tangle.

Thread it easy!

Does arthritis, unsteady hands, or vision impairment make needle threading difficult for you? If so, you can solve the problem with a slotted needle, sometimes called a handicapped needle.

slot

Available in sizes 80, 90, and 100, this needle features a slot in the side of the eye. To thread, hold the strand of thread firmly to the side of the needle and pass the thread along the needle shaft until it slips through the slot and into the eye.

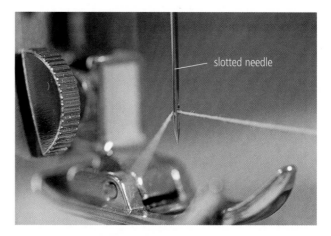

slotted needle

> ✉ **Note:** Because the eye is slotted, this needle is more fragile than a standard needle of comparable size, so be gentle when threading and handling.

Quick needle changes

It's important to use the proper size and type of needle in your sewing machine and serger. Here are some ideas for fumble-free needle changing.

• Use magnetized tweezers to hold the needle you're removing from the machine—and then the new needle you're inserting.

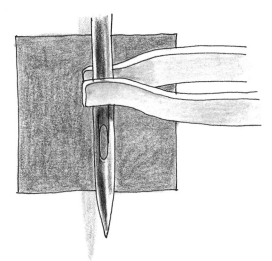

Magnetized tweezers

• Before removing the needle, thread it with a short length of thread and knot this thread behind and in front of the needle eye. Use this thread as a handle—you'll never lose even the most slippery needle. Clip the thread to remove it when the needle is in place.

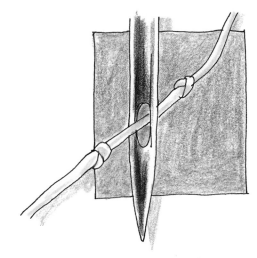

Knotted thread

• Insert a very fine hand-sewing needle through the eye of the machine needle. This extra holder will allow you to guide the needle effortlessly into position.

Needle

Thread tamers

To use large cones of thread on your conventional sewing machine without a thread holder, cut off the bottom of a two-liter soda bottle, pass the thread through the top opening, and place the bottle over the cone and behind your machine. This also works great for unruly yarn balls used for decorative serging.

QUICK
CLOSURES

Zippers, buttons, hooks—those artful, yet functional

garment details—can be very time consuming to

sew by hand. Learn how to save time by applying

fasteners by machine.

CLOSE ENCOUNTERS

Speed up the process of applying closures using the tips in this chapter.

And discover some creative uses for ordinary notions.

Zippers

You can't find a quicker closure than a zipper. And with these tricks, inserting them will be a snap.

Shortening zippers

Sometimes you just can't find a zipper in the right size, and you don't want to disrupt your sewing with a trip to the fabric store. Shortening a zipper you have in your stash is a quick and simple process.

Jacket zippers

You can shorten separating zippers only at the upper end, so stitch the zipper into the jacket according to instructions, allowing the excess length to extend at the neckline edge.

1. Partially open the zipper, and place the slider 2" below the desired length to avoid detaching the slider. If your zipper has a metal stop at the upper end, remove it with pliers and reposition it at the new length. If the stop is molded plastic, create another stop by whipstitching over the coil or teeth at the new length on each side of the zipper.

2. Cut away the excess zipper tape ¾" above the new stop, and finish the jacket.

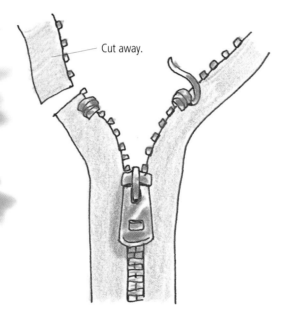

Cut away.

Shortening separating zipper

Skirt zippers

Depending on your preference, you can shorten nonseparating zippers at either the upper end or the lower end.

To shorten a zipper from the upper end:

1. Install the zipper, positioning the lower end stop at the garment placket opening lower edge.

2. Open the zipper to avoid accidentally cutting off the zipper slider.

3. Stitch across the zipper tape within the top seam allowance; cut off the excess zipper.

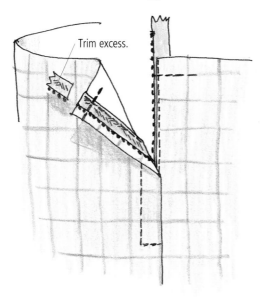

Shortening skirt zipper from top

4. Continue constructing the garment; the waistband or facing will serve as the zipper upper end stop.

To shorten a zipper from the lower end:

1. Mark the desired finished length from the top end stop of the zipper.

2. Make a new lower end stop; whipstitch by hand or zigzag by machine over the zipper teeth at the desired length.

3. Cut off the zipper ½" below the new lower end stop.

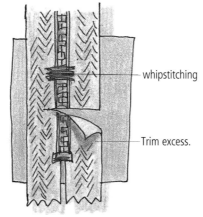

Shortening skirt zipper from bottom

4. Install the zipper.

Quick pick

One of the details that separates couture from the homemade look is a hand-picked zipper. Those even stitches hand sewn on each side of the zipper identify that garment as well made—and requiring lots of time.

If handstitching isn't your forte, take heart! Your sewing machine can give you the look of handstitching, with the precision only a machine can afford. Use the blindhem stitch and the following technique:

1. Buy a zipper (preferably with a tricot-like tape) that's at least 1" longer than the pattern suggests.

2. Using chalk or an air-soluble marker, mark the zipper lower end opening on the garment seamline.

3. Beginning at the garment lower end, stitch the seam to the marking, and then backstitch.

4. Loosen the upper thread tension and lengthen the stitch to baste the remainder of the seam. Return the thread tension to normal.

5. Position the closed zipper facedown, centering the teeth over the seamline, with the zipper pull extending at least 1" beyond the garment upper edge.

6. Using extra-long straight pins (quilting pins), pin the zipper from the wrong side so the pins enter the zipper tape and fabric ¼" from the teeth, run under the zipper teeth, and exit ¼" beyond the other side of the teeth; position the pins 1" apart.

7. Set your sewing machine for a 2mm- to 2.5mm-wide blindhem stitch with a stitch length of 2mm. If your blindhem foot has a narrow toe on the left, use it; if not, use your zipper foot.

8. Fold the seam allowance back to the point where the pins enter the fabric so the zipper is underneath the work.

Pin zipper in place.

9. Removing the pins before stitching over them, blindstitch along the edge of the exposed fold so the straight stitches are positioned on the seam allowance and catch the zipper tape and the zigzag stitches barely "bite" into the fabric fold.

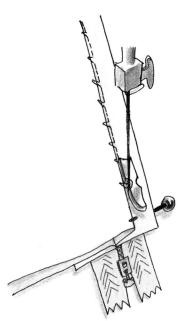

Blindstitched "hand-picked" zipper

10. Repeat for the remaining side of the zipper. Note where the first zigzag stitch has "bitten" into the fold on the first side and set your machine so the "bite" stitch on the second side is directly across from the first side.

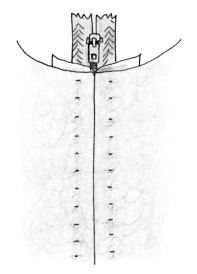

Garment right side

11. Lightly press the zipper flat and remove the seamline basting stitches.

12. Anchor the zipper tape lower end to the seam allowance by hand. Move the zipper pull to the zipper lower end. Stitch the facing or waistband to the garment, catching the zipper upper end in the seam.

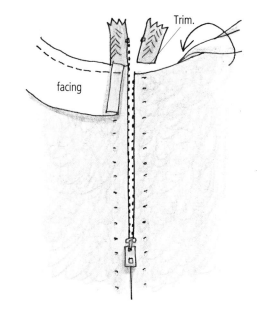

Attach facing.

13. With the zipper open, cut the zipper upper edge off even with the waistband or facing seam allowance.

> ✉ **Note:** Before inserting your garment's zipper, practice the above steps a few times on extra fabric using an old zipper until the tiny stitches show uniformly on the right side.

Slider smart

• If a metal zipper won't remain zipped while the garment is being worn, give it a good shot of hair spray, being careful to protect the garment fabric while spraying.

• If your zipper doesn't slide smoothly, rub the teeth with pencil lead, or spray with a nonstick cooking spray such as PAM™.

• Avoid the "blip" (wide spot) when stitching around the zipper pull by using a zipper longer than the pattern suggests for the placket opening. Slide the zipper pull above the garment, complete the zipper stitching, unzip the zipper, and cut off the excess tape length.

• To reuse a zipper from a discarded garment, remove it and then apply spray starch.

• Help children dress themselves by adding ribbons or decorative baubles to the zipper pull, making it easier for small hands to manipulate.

On the edge

The zipper, a simple, functional closure mechanism, takes on a new look when used as a trim. Often sold by the yard, metal-tooth zipper tape makes the perfect sporty edge finish for hair bows, jackets, and pockets—wherever a piped edge is appropriate.

Zipper trim

For a zipper edge:

1. Unzip the preshrunk tape length, and use each half like piping.

2. With right sides together, match the tape woven edge to the seamline raw edge.

3. Using a zipper foot, baste close to the zipper teeth.

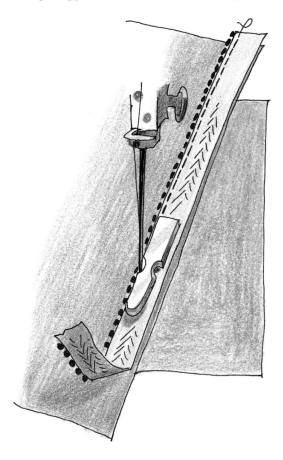

Baste zipper in place.

4. With the basting line as your stitching guide, join the seam, enclosing the zipper tape and leaving only the teeth to add glitz to the project right side.

Zany zippers

Zip together separating zipper halves of two different colors and use as a design feature on sportswear.

Choose your child's school colors or stark black and white, or create a holiday favorite using red and green or black and orange combos.

Hooks

Sewing on fasteners with the machine saves time and tedium—no more dropped hooks lost forever.

1. Set the stitch length on your machine to zero, or lower the feed dogs.
2. Using a button foot (or no foot at all), attach the hooks in place with a zigzag stitch, adjusting the stitch width as needed to accommodate the hole spacing.

Machine-stitching hooks

3. If you're attaching multiple hooks, just keep sewing—there's no need to cut threads between them.
4. Clip all thread ends and secure each with a drop of seam sealant.

Hook-and-loop fasteners

Because of its endless versatility, hook-and-loop fastener tape, such as Velcro™, is one of today's most widely used closures. It works anywhere two edges overlap—just let the two halves touch, and the hooks and loops immediately interlock for a secure closure.

This sewing notion is usually much faster to apply than traditional closures like hooks and eyes or buttons and buttonholes. Available as strip yardage and in circles and squares, in sew-on, adhesive-backed, and iron-on versions, hook-and-loop fasteners are popular not only for sportswear and home decorating, but for children's clothing and fashion accessories as well.

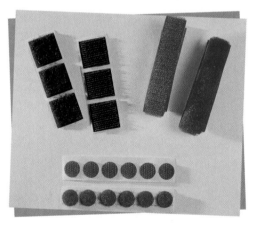

To attach all types of hook-and-loop tape:
• Place the hook portion of the tape so that it faces outward on the garment and away from the body; place the loop portion facing inward.
• Angle the tape corners to eliminate sharp points.

✉ **Note:** Close the hook-and-loop tape when washing or dry-cleaning to prevent the hooks from snagging other clothing and to keep lint from collecting in the hooks.

To attach sew-on hook-and-loop tape:

• Use a glue stick to position the tape.

• Choose a size 90 or 100 sewing machine needle.

• Sew the tape very close to the edge with a stitch length of 8 to 10 stitches per inch (2.5mm to 3mm long).

• When sewing a strip, begin near the center of one long edge center and stitch around the tape, overlapping stitches at the beginning and end.

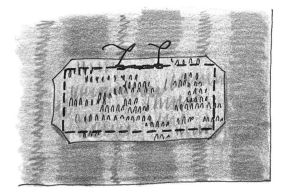

Stitch around edges.

• When attaching circles of hook-and-loop tape, stitch in a triangle or square shape.

Stitch in square or triangle shape.

Buttons

These closures can be practical or fun, round or square, and any color or shape under the sun.

Sew on a button without a knot

Eliminating small tasks like tying a knot can mean big time savings—especially if you have several buttons to attach.

> ✉ **Note:** Run your thread through beeswax to help strengthen it and prevent tangles.

1. Mark the button position.

2. Thread the needle with a double strand of thread.

3. Insert the needle on the garment underside, about 1" from the button position. Tunnel it between the fabric layers, bringing the needle up at the button position. Take a few backstitches to lock the thread.

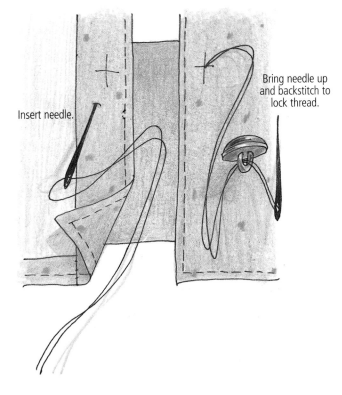

Insert needle.

Bring needle up and backstitch to lock thread.

Knotless thread

4. To allow for some extra play on sew-through buttons, insert a toothpick or small crochet hook between the button and the fabric. Bring the needle through the button and back down into the fabric. Repeat, bringing the needle up, through the button, and back down into the fabric four or five more times.

5. To form the thread shank, remove the toothpick or crochet hook and wind the thread around the extra length underneath the button. Draw the needle to the garment underside and fasten with several tiny backstitches.

6. Now insert the needle into the fabric and tunnel it between the layers for about 1". Bring the needle out on the garment underside. Clip the beginning and ending threads close to the fabric. If the garment is a single layer or the fabric is sheer, clip the thread close to the backstitches instead of tunneling it.

Sturdy strands

It's late at night and you've reached the last step on your new coat—attaching the buttons. If, after scouring the thread rack, you can't find the appropriate heavy-duty thread color, don't despair. Head for your needlework drawer and substitute embroidery floss in the correct color. Using multiple floss strands will keep your coat buttons securely attached.

Button whims

If those buttons you can't live without aren't washable, and removing them every time you dry-clean is out of the question, try button pins. These specially designed pins allow you to pin and unpin your buttons, saving you time and tedious resewing.

Shaped like a safety pin with a bump on one side, the button pin body hides on the garment wrong side, while the bump secures the button shank on the garment right side.

Next time you get a yen to change buttons for a whole new look, make it easy and just pin!

Button buffers

Another way to protect fragile buttons is to make protective covers.

1. Cut a piece of sew-in (not adhesive) hook-and-loop tape slightly larger than your button.

2. Make a slit in the hook portion long enough for the button to fit through.

3. When the loop side is pressed in place, the button will be sandwiched between the layers, protected from damage during the laundering process.

Back that button

A backer button, also called a stay button, is the clear, flat, two-holed button used to reinforce the area under a fashion button, eliminating strain on the fabric and helping to prevent the fashion button from pulling out.

Backer buttons are available in four sizes, ranging from ⅜" to ¾" in diameter. Or you can use any small flat button. When selecting a backer button, consider the weight of the fabric and the amount of stress on the button. As a general rule, use backer buttons when you sew fashion buttons on heavy fabric or on a single layer of fabric. Use them on coats and jackets and when working with boiled wool, leather, suede, vinyl, or knits.

To apply a backer button:

1. Place the backer button on the inside of the garment under the fashion button.

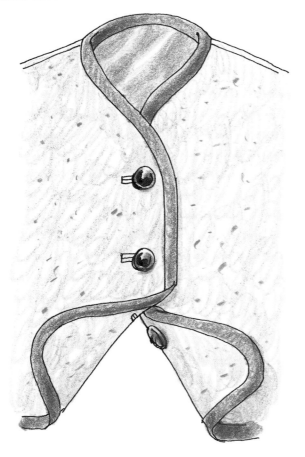

Backer button

2. Sew through the backer button at the same time you sew on the fashion button.

3. If the fashion button needs a thread shank, form the shank between the fashion button and the fabric.

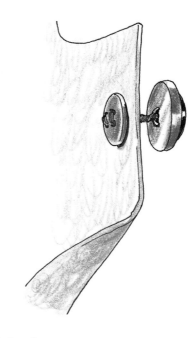

Thread shank

Button, button . . .

Take your fashion cue from designers who transform the ordinary into the extraordinary with a fashion accessory that can be found at your local fabric store—the button cover.

A basic blouse rises to many occasions with the use of simple-to-make button covers. Choose a rhinestone set for evening, or pop on a jet-black set for a more tailored look. Go funky with a set of button covers in related patterns—for example, a black and white combo in plaids, stripes, dots, and checks (one of each). Or go crazier yet by marching the traffic signal colors of red, yellow, and green up your shirtfront.

The possibilities are endless, and creating your own button cover set requires only a little glue and some imagination.

Clever cuffs

Buttons disguised as cuff links are making their way into the jewelry boxes of many smart fashion sewers. These links are quick and easy to make and are less costly than ready-mades.

• Choose four matching buttons with wire or self-shanks.

Shank buttons

• Position two buttons back to back and stitch a ⅜"-long thread shank between them, using a blanket stitch.

Thread shank

• Secure the stitching with a drop of seam sealant. Repeat, using the remaining two buttons for the other cuff link.

If thread shanks aren't to your liking, connect the buttons with cuff-link connector pins from a fabric or craft store. To use:

• Gently twist the connector loop ends in opposite directions; slip a button on each loop and twist the pin back to its original shape.

Cuff-link connector pin

• Using needle-nosed pliers, gently crimp the loops so the buttons won't shift.

Insert your designer jewels into the cuffs of your favorite shirt or blouse and stand back to enjoy the compliments.

Buttonhole safety

Buttonholes are usually the last step in garment construction. One slip of the seam ripper at this point can be disastrous.

To cut open your buttonholes without worrying about cutting through the ends and ruining your garment, follow this simple technique:

1. Complete the buttonhole stitching, tie off all threads, and dot with seam sealant.

2. Place a straight pin across each bartack end.

3. Using your seam ripper or small scissors, pierce the buttonhole center and cut toward each end. The straight pin will prevent you from cutting through the end of your stitching.

Loop scoop

Button-and-loop closures add designer appeal to any sewn creation. Whether you're making a sleek wool jersey suit or a one-of-a-kind wedding gown, you can add these loops with little ado.

Well-made button loops are round, firm, and equal in size and thickness. Depending on the fabric's weight and texture, button loops can be from $\frac{1}{32}$" to $\frac{1}{4}$" in diameter. For easier, more attractive button loops, use this designer technique:

1. Cut a bias fabric strip 1" to $1\frac{1}{4}$" wide.

2. With right sides together, fold the strip in half lengthwise; stitch close to the folded edge, stitching the beginning slightly wider for easier turning.

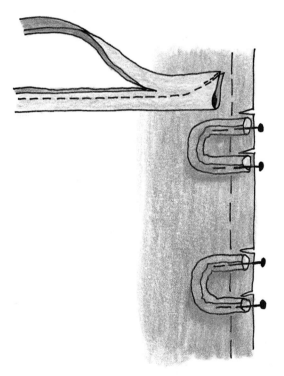

Button-loop closures

> ✉ **Note:** To prevent popped stitches later, stretch the fabric as much as possible while stitching.

3. Trim the seam allowances, leaving enough excess to "self-cord" the button loop; the amount you leave will depend on the fabric weight. Make a test loop to determine the ideal amount.

4. Use a tapestry needle, bodkin, loop turner, or Fasturn® to turn the tube.

5. For skinny loops without lumps and bumps, thoroughly wet the strip and squeeze it dry in a towel. Pin one end of the tube to the ironing board, stretch the tubing as much as possible without twisting the seamline, and then pin the other end to the ironing board; let the tube dry.

Positioning loops

When sewing the button loops into a garment/facing seam:

1. Determine the desired finished length of each loop (long enough to fit over the button without strain) and then add $1\frac{1}{4}$" for seam allowances.

2. Cut a test loop. Hold $\frac{5}{8}$" at each end of the loop and then insert the button through the loop; adjust as necessary. Cut the desired number of loops of the correct length.

3. To determine the space between loops, add two times the width of the tube to the button diameter. Clip into the garment seam allowance to mark the top and bottom of each loop. On the right side of the garment, pin the loop ends in place at the clips so the tube seamline is centered.

4. Recheck loop spacing and size, and then baste on the seamline. With right sides together, join the facing and the garment. Tack the ends of the loops to the interfacing.

5. Turn the garment right side out; then understitch as usual for blouses or dresses. Do not understitch jackets and coats.

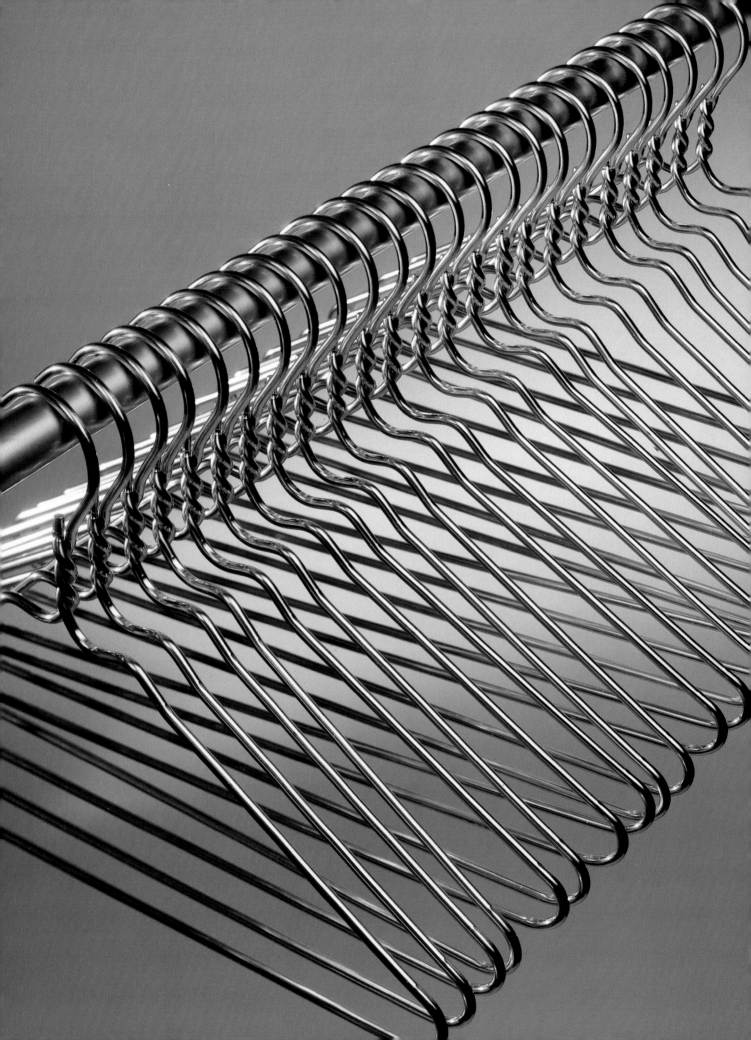

TAKE CARE

After spending time and money sewing

a great wardrobe, you'll want to keep it looking like new.

Remember—proper care means longer wear.

TO CLEAN OR NOT TO CLEAN

Add life to your wardrobe by following the best

cleaning method for each type of fabric. And find out how to prevent

as well as remove stains.

Fabric first

Taking care of your clothing actually begins when you purchase the fabric. Read the labels on fabric bolts and refer to the industry's standard chart below for care instructions.

Fabric care labeling

1. Machine wash warm
2. Machine wash warm, line dry
3. Machine wash warm, tumble dry, remove promptly
4. Machine wash warm, delicate cycle, tumble dry low, use cool iron
5. Machine wash warm, do not dry-clean
6. Hand wash separately, use cool iron
7. Dry-clean only
8. Dry-clean pile fabric method only
9. Wipe with damp cloth only
10. Machine wash warm, tumble dry or line dry

Be sure to preshrink wools (including lambswool), angora, and cashmere. Then dry-clean garments, which is less likely than laundering to cause shrinkage.

Without proper care, some silk dyes bleed or fade. Silk is susceptible to shrinkage, and the fibers may split or shred in a close-fitting garment.

Genuine suede and leather garments require special cleaning to maintain the feel and color. Always have suede cleaned by a qualified professional. Dark suedes and leather trim may bleed onto an adjoining lighter fabric or leather. Because the tanning process stretches skins, shrinkage may occur gradually over time.

Not all fabrics are suitable for dry-cleaning. Bonded fabrics (where the face of the fabric is chemically adhered to a lining fabric) may separate from backings during dry-cleaning, and the glued backings on some belts can dissolve or become brittle.

Plastic buttons and sequins may soften or dissolve in dry-cleaning fluid.

On the spot

According to Murphy's Law, the first time you wear a beautiful new creation you will spill coffee (or something) all over it. If you attend to a spill or other mishap promptly, you'll find your garment will maintain its newness longer.

Stain prevention

Your mother was right: you can prevent most stains just by being a bit more careful. This doesn't mean that your clothes must always be compatible with what you're eating—but you can try to wear the right clothes for the occasion.

• Change from your work attire to casual clothes as soon as you arrive home, especially before cooking or cleaning the house.

• Wear an apron or coverall during activities likely to produce stains. A lab coat is great for throwing on over your business attire for last-minute duties, such as feeding children or taking out the trash, before heading for work.

• Save worn-out clothes for really messy jobs like painting and car repair. Don't even bother to remove spots from these. Wash them once in a while (by themselves), or just throw them out when the job is complete.

• Wear cotton undergarments to keep perspiration off your clothes. Undergarments such as camisoles protect the entire bodice or shirt area.

• Apply perfume before getting dressed; some perfumes affect fabric dyes.

• Resist using shoe polish or a felt-tip pen to touch up handbags and belts; the polish and ink can rub off onto your clothes.

• To avoid metal stains, hang clothing on plastic or padded hangers. Keep metal jewelry and accessories polished, and promptly remove safety pins.

• Make it a habit to check clothes as you take them off—before they are washed or dry-cleaned—so you can treat spots as soon as possible; the older the spot, the harder it is to remove.

• Never iron (or use hot water on) clothes that have absorbed dirt or perspiration; heat sets stains.

Emergency measures

• Remove solid matter such as food by gently scraping with a dull knife, the edge of a teaspoon, a nail file, or a toothbrush. Allow mud to dry, and then scrape it off.

• Blot liquid spills with a clean rag or cloth napkin. If cloth items aren't available, use a paper napkin (do not rub the fabric with a paper napkin, as it will leave lint). For best results, first lay the affected area over a clean cloth. Then, using another clean cloth, blot from the center to the edges to prevent rings, lifting the blotting cloth up and down to avoid spreading the liquid.

• Absorb grease spills with flour, cornstarch, or plain talcum powder (keep a small bottle in your purse). Sprinkle the powder on evenly and shake or brush it off when dry; repeat if necessary.

• Flush nongreasy spills from washable fabrics with cool water.

• If you prick your finger while sewing and leave a tiny blood spot on your project, moisten a cloth or paper towel with cool water and press it against the spot until the blood is absorbed.

• Check the area after emergency treatment. If the spot is still there, retreat it within the next day or two.

Stock up for spot removal

Most of what you need for removing spots you probably already have around the house. Look for these supplies at a supermarket, drugstore, or hardware store.

• Scraping tool such as a dull knife, teaspoon, or nail file

• Plastic squeeze bottles and set of plastic measuring spoons for mixing solutions

• Clean white rags

• Toothbrush

- Absorbent powder, such as cornstarch or plain (non-cosmetic) talcum powder, for treating grease and oils on nonwashables
- Solvents, such as bar laundry soap, white vinegar, household ammonia, and rubbing alcohol, for treating grease and oils on washables
- Trichloroethane or trichloroethylene-type dry-cleaning fluid for removing grease
- Eyedropper, cotton swabs, and small sponge for applying liquid solvents

- Liquid laundry detergent for water-based spots
- Enzyme presoak for protein-based spots
- Lubricant, such as glycerin, coconut oil, or mineral (baby) oil, for organic spots
- Bleach, such as lemon juice, hydrogen peroxide, or commercial oxygen bleach, for use as a last resort

> ✎ **Note:** Remember that many cleaning materials are toxic. Keep them out of reach of children.

Basic procedures

Follow these general guidelines before attempting to remove any spots:
- Read the cleaning product labels and take any precautions necessary for the garment or yourself.
- Never use enzyme presoaks for silk, wool, or animal fur because these products will cause damage if left on for more than a few minutes.

- Be aware that bleach can damage dyes and fibers.
- Oils and alcohols are flammable, so don't use or store them near an open flame.
- Some cleaners may cause skin irritation, so wear plastic gloves for protection.
- If you splash anything at all in your eyes, rinse them immediately with cold running water.
- Avoid breathing the fumes emitted by dry-cleaning fluid.
- Don't use dry-cleaning fluid if you've been drinking an alcoholic beverage.
- Don't mix cleaners unless recommended to do so by a reliable source.

When applying dry-cleaning fluid, lubricants, or bleach:

1. Test the cleaner in a hidden area such as a seam allowance first.

2. Place a folded rag under the spot to absorb soil and protect the rest of the garment. Change this rag between treatments.

3. Gently rub a small amount of cleaner onto the fabric with a cotton swab; don't scrub. Use as little cleaner as possible, rather than soaking the area.

4. Wait a minute or two and then blot. If the fabric's color and texture don't change and no dye is visible on the blotter, the cleaner is probably safe. Should the dye begin to run, immediately rinse the spot with water (if using dry-cleaning fluid, let it evaporate).

5. If the treatment is working, but slowly, repeat one or more times.

6. Thoroughly flush out cleaner (or allow dry-cleaning fluid to evaporate) after spot removal or before trying another treatment.

7. When the spot is gone, sandwich the treated area between folded rags, blot, and then let dry.

8. Don't apply heat to speed drying.

FIX IT FAST

Even the best-made clothes need repairs from time to time.

All of the products mentioned for the following repair techniques are readily available

from notions departments, fabric stores, and sewing supply

mail-order catalogs.

Plan ahead

Each time you complete a garment, save any leftover fabrics and notions. Extra buttons, leftover thread, fabric scraps, and assorted findings such as stray sequins and beads make later repairs much easier.

Set up notebooks or card files for recording fiber content and care requirements and for storing actual samples. The more clothing you sew and the more people you sew for, the more useful such a system is likely to be.

Missing buttons

For quick and easy button replacement, save the extra buttons when you sew a new garment. If no matching buttons are available, try mixing buttons. Use assorted big buttons on a coat front for a designer detail, or dress up a plain shirt or blouse with related jeweled buttons. If match you must, steal a button from an inconspicuous place on the garment, such as the lowermost button on a blouse. You could remove the cuff buttons and replace them with decorative buttons (mock cuff links), or rob the upper-

most button and replace it with a fancy button as a mock brooch.

For fast, temporary repairs, keep some emergency buttons on hand. One type of emergency button has two parts; to attach, push the prong of this shirt button look-alike through the buttonhole and into the backing-disk hole. Another type of emergency button resembles the plastic tie used to attach price tags.

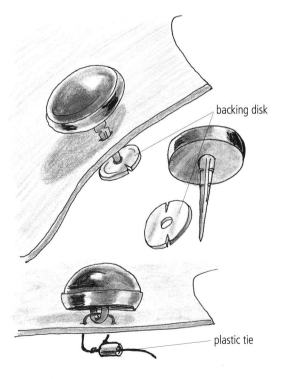

backing disk

plastic tie

Emergency buttons

Snags

Don't cut off the loose thread or yarn loop on a snagged sweater, a knit garment, or loosely woven fabric—you'll just create a hole. Instead, pull the snag through to the wrong side. A small plastic crochet hook does the job beautifully, but there are also tiny latch-hook tools specially designed for this quick repair.

Quick fix

You can't beat double-face, self-stick tape for quick and temporary repairs. Use it to tack up a loose hem, fasten an errant shoulder pad, close an embarrassing gap between bodice buttons, or keep a wrap skirt wrapped.

Cut a few 3"- to 4"-long pieces of double-face tape to keep in your wallet or pack in your suitcase—instant bandages for clothes.

Stain smarts

If you're faced with a permanent stain, it's time to get creative.

Cover the stain with rows of trim, a patch pocket or two, or an artful appliqué. Appliqués made from luxurious fabrics such as synthetic suede, polyester silkies, or lace may actually make your garment look even better.

Brush a light coat of sparkling fabric paint over the damaged area, or add a monogram. Repeat any decorative treatments elsewhere on the garment for balance and harmony—make it look as if you meant to embellish the garment in the first place.

Darn it

Darning is an old-fashioned form of repair that you can do quickly on today's programmable sewing machines. Some computerized machines let you sew a row of stitches, push a button to record the information, and then automatically sew duplicate rows back and forth across the area that needs darning. Some machines will darn sideways as well as forward and backward so you don't even have to turn the work. Top models offer several mending and darning stitch patterns for different weights of woven fabrics and knits.

You can darn using a basic machine, too; you'll just have to reposition the fabric for each row of stitches. If the spot you're darning is threadbare, baste a layer of self-fabric, lightweight fabric, or sheer tricot to the wrong side of the worn area before you start. Then use a straight, three-step zigzag, or honeycomb stitch, also called a smocking stitch, to cover the area. Trim the reinforcing fabric close to the darning stitches when you're finished.

More mending methods

Darning is strong and durable, but it can be conspicuous. If you prefer a less obvious mend, use fusible products and one of these three techniques:

Same-fabric patch
1. Trim the frayed threads from the damaged fabric edges.
2. Fuse a patch of self-fabric over the damaged area wrong side. A potential drawback: if the repair is large the mended area will be crisper than the rest of the garment.

Tricot or interfacing patch

To preserve the garment's drape and hold frayed edges together, use fusible tricot or fusible, nonwoven sheer interfacing. This works not only for general tears, but especially for a stressed seam that has popped open and shredded the fabric around the stitches.

1. Remove the stitches along the damaged seam.

2. Cut two strips of fusible tricot or fusible, nonwoven sheer interfacing slightly larger than the damaged area, rounding the corners; fuse one strip to each side of the damaged seam.

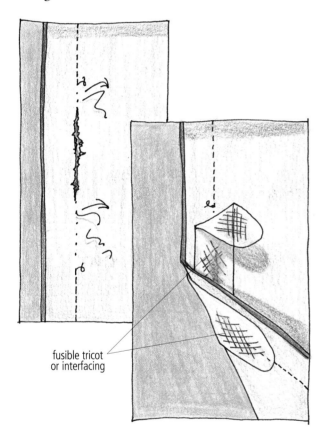

fusible tricot
or interfacing

Repair stressed seam.

3. Restitch the seam.

Paperhanger's patch

This method is a variation of a technique used by paperhangers to patch holes in wallpaper. The patch can be practically invisible.

1. Lay a scrap of matching fabric over the damaged area, matching any pattern lines.

2. Use a craft knife to cut an oval or round patch through both layers at once.

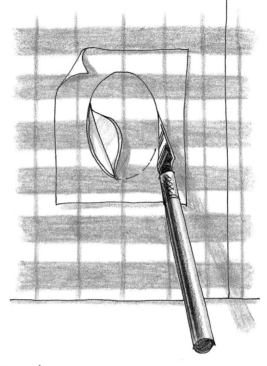

Cut patch.

3. From the wrong side, remove the damaged fabric.

4. On the wrong side, place a larger oval of fusible tricot or nonwoven sheer interfacing over the patched area. Fuse the tricot and matching fabric in place at the same time. The patch will blend from the right side.

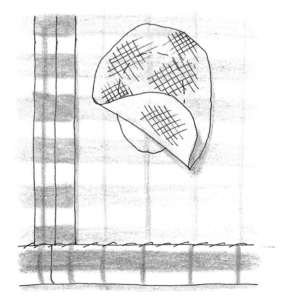

Fuse patch in place.

Slit splits

"Car wash" hemlines and other styles with slits are weakest at the slit's upper point—the point at which the seam ends.

If the fabric has shredded, cover the damage with an embroidered arrowhead. Many programmable sewing machines have a motif stitch pattern for this purpose. Or you can purchase a small arrowhead appliqué. Using a little bit of fabric glue, adhere the arrowhead to the garment right side at the slit upper edge. Then straight stitch around the edges.

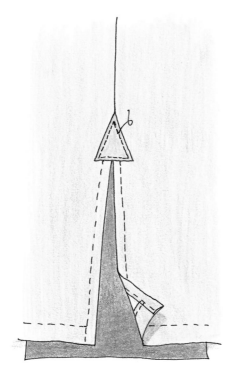

Arrowhead appliqué

Patch as patch can

If you lived through the Depression and patched out of necessity, you might be surprised by the aesthetic appeal of patches. You can group decorative patches for an artistic touch or scatter them randomly throughout. Either way, decorative patching is a quick fix for tears or holes in otherwise good garments. Teenagers especially love the look.

To patch, use fusible transfer web to hold shapes in place, and then accent the patches with decorative edgestitching, either by hand or by machine. To tie in patches with the garment design, add coordinating stitching to pockets, collars, or closures.

Mending holes in sweaters

For the quickest and most durable repair for a hole in a sweater, sew two rows of machine stitching around the hole plus a few rows of machine darning across it. Other methods, though not as quick, are neater.

If the sweater has begun to run, reknit the loops with a crochet hook. Pass the hook through a loose loop and reach around the undone yarn in the row of knit stitches above it.

For the stockinette pattern shown, the hook pulls the crosswise yarn through the loop and creates a new loose loop in the higher row. Repeat until you have reknit every undone yarn above the loose loop.

For garter-stitch knits, insert the crochet hook from the back of the sweater on one row and from the front on the next.

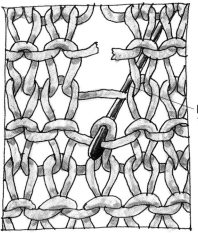

Insert hook from back.

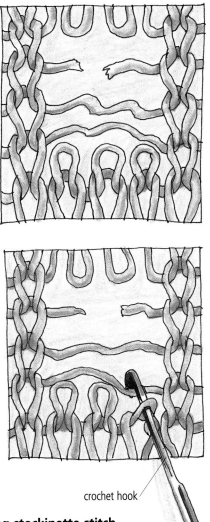

crochet hook

Mending stockinette stitch

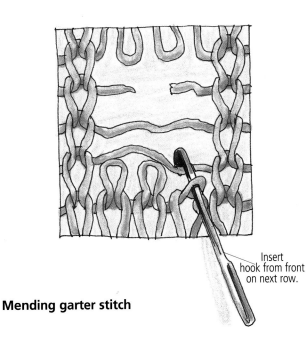

Insert hook from front on next row.

Mending garter stitch

Most knit patterns can be mended with variations of these two techniques. Look carefully at the stitch pattern and reknit one stitch at a time. If it doesn't look right, undo it and try inserting the crochet hook from the opposite side.

When all undone crosswise yarns have been reknit, hand sew through the remaining loose loops and around the broken yarns close to the hole to prevent future runs. If you need to close a fairly large area, sew with matching yarn and a yarn needle. To match the yarn weight of the sweater, you can separate heavy yarn into single plies.

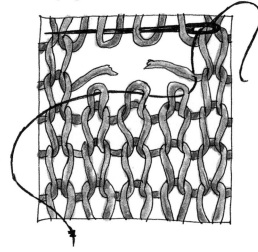

Sewing through loose loops

If the sweater hole occurs where one or two different-colored yarns have been broken, sew the loops together with clear or smoke-colored monofilament thread.

Leave a 2" thread length at the beginning and end of hand mending, and then knot the ends together on the sweater wrong side when the fix is completed.

Lace repair

Knowing how to do a quick mend on lace may come in handy at a wedding or other important occasion. The same sewing techniques will repair a tear in an heirloom gown, a collar on a young girl's dress or replace the stained area of a tablecloth with a matching lace insert.

Before beginning to sew, clean the lace if possible, especially if it's old. Baste delicate lace to muslin, wash in lukewarm water with mild detergent, and dry flat. To restore cotton or linen lace to its original shape, pin it to an ironing board to dry.

To join lace edges, overcast by hand on the motif or on the illusion (tulle background). However, the lace is strongest if stitches are anchored to heavier areas.

Overcasting edges

Use no knots. Instead, make a few backstitches at the beginning and end of the work, preferably within the flower area. If the lace is old, delicate, or under stress, back it with a strip of nylon tulle in a matching color. Overcast the tulle at both sides of the tear line, and the handstitches will disappear into the lace.

There are five popular lace patterns, all of which can be cut and sewn with little raveling.

• **Chantilly lace** features a rose design over a tulle background. When trimming this lace, cut around the flower edges.

Chantilly lace

• **Alençon lace** has a flower pattern outlined with a heavier, raised thread. This reembroidery produces a rich look. If you trim the background, the flower can be used as an appliqué. When trimming, do not cut through the heavy outline thread.

Alençon lace

• **Rose point or Venice lace**, sometimes made of silk, contains no illusion. Cut any of the joining threads, called tie bars.

Rose point or Venice lace

• **Cluny lace** is usually made of cotton and somewhat resembles crochet. It has a great tendency to ravel. You can cut it anywhere in the pattern. Reinforce cut ends with a few handstitches. For raveling areas, rework the pattern with a small crochet hook or remove the damaged spot and insert new lace.

Cluny lace

• **Schiffli lace** is another type of embroidered lace. Cut only the illusion area on this type of lace.

Schiffli lace

FRESH DRESSING

Keep your clothes looking like new—day in and day out, in town and out—

by following these hints for cleaning, repair, and packing.

Secrets for a sparkling wardrobe

Here are some tips for keeping your clothes looking like new:

• To prevent embarrassing moments, mend all loose seams and replace or reinforce buttons when you first notice a problem.

• Air recently worn but unsoiled clothes overnight before hanging them back in your closet.

• Remove stains promptly. If the garment is washable, soak it in cool water immediately; if not, check the fabric fiber content and treat accordingly.

• Give knit clothes new life by removing any pilling with a garment shaver or fabric comb.

• When laundering a garment, wash matching fabric belts or sashes at the same time for consistent color loss.

• Wash and dry-clean clothes only as often as really necessary. Overcleaning can be harmful to fabrics.

• Give away any garment you don't feel good wearing—it's good for your morale, and another person may love wearing something "new."

• Replace elastic that has lost its shape.

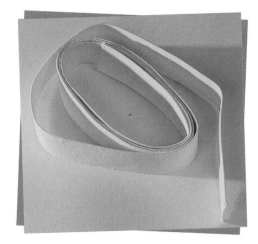

Underarm protection

Designed to keep garments fresh and reduce dry-cleaning bills, dress shields also protect clothes from perspiration and deodorant stains. You can buy dress shields. But why not custom-make shields to fit your wardrobe? They're quick, easy, and inexpensive to sew.

Dress shields are made of two layers of fabric. Use an absorbent fabric such as handkerchief linen, cotton batiste, flannel, or lightweight silk next to the skin and self-fabric or a fabric in a flesh color next to the garment. If you perspire heavily, insert an inner layer of cotton flannel for more absorption.

To make a dress shield:

1. Pin the garment front and back pattern pieces together at the underarm seam.

2. Trace onto tissue paper the armhole cutting line between the front and back notches. Mark a point on the underarm seam 4" from the traced line. Draw the curved lower edge of the shield connecting the notches.

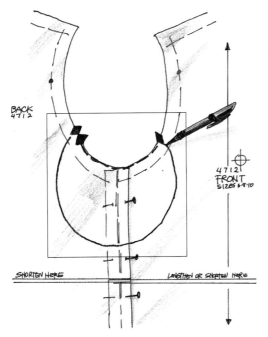

Making dress shield pattern

3. For garments with sleeves, cut four shield pieces from self-fabric and four from absorbent fabric. Cut two pieces of each fabric for sleeveless garments.

4. With right sides together, stitch two pieces at the underarm with a ¼" seam to make one section. Repeat until all sections are stitched.

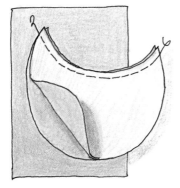

Stitching underarm seam

5. Place two sections right sides together. Stitch around outer edge with a ¼" seam, leaving a 2" opening on one side for turning. Repeat to make a pair. Turn shields right side out and edgestitch openings.

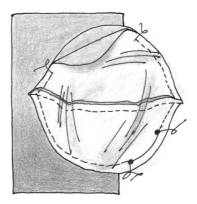

Joining dress shield halves

6. Trim the garment armhole seams between the notches to ¼". Tack or snap the shields in place at the seamlines.

Wrinkle-free wardrobing

Who wants to iron when she could be sewing? Follow the hints below to keep clothes looking fresh and wrinkle free:

• Choose knits and loosely woven, textured fabrics with crease-resistant finishes.

• For wardrobe basics, choose fabrics in dark colors and prints, which tend to camouflage wrinkles.

• Hang up clothes when you take them off.

• To remove wrinkles from wool garments, hang them in the bathroom while you shower.

• Make your clothing choices the night before and hang the garments outside the closet; many wrinkles will fall out overnight.

• Wash knits and permanent press clothes on your machine's delicate cycle and remove them before the final spin; hang to dry. Or remove clothes from the dryer before they're completely dry, and hang them up. You'll notice fewer wrinkles.

Five steps to perfect packing

If you're a frequent traveler, you probably know that packing smart saves wear and tear on road clothes, the clothes you always take on trips because they're comfortable and require little ironing, and that you feel good in.

Packing a suitcase is a special art. Follow these packing steps and you should arrive at your destination with clean, wrinkle-free clothes.

1. Pack all your heavier items—shoes, handbags, hair dryer—at the bottom of the suitcase. Shoe toe space is perfect for any small crushable items. Cover shoes with plastic to avoid getting polish or dirt on clothing.

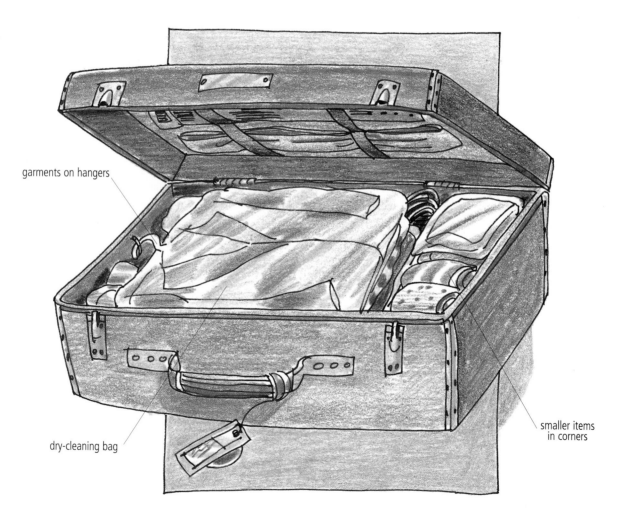

garments on hangers

dry-cleaning bag

smaller items in corners

2. When folding sweaters or sweatshirts, fold both sleeves across the front (or back) of the garment body, and then fold the garment hem area up to the neckline. Fold knit pants and skirts as usual. Pack these clothes on top of the heavier items.

3. Empty pockets, fasten closures, and remove belts and jewelry from all other garments.

4. Place one, two, or three garments on a lightweight hanger (pants/blouse/jacket is a nice combination) and cover them with a dry-cleaning bag. This will take up additional room, but it will trap air around each garment and help prevent wrinkles. If you have the luxury of space, pack each garment on an individual hanger and in a separate dry-cleaning bag. Pad fragile garments, such as silk blouses, with a few sheets of tissue paper to further cushion the folding.

Beginning with heavier items such as jackets and pants, layer the clothing in the dry-cleaning bags, allowing the hanger portion of each to hang out of the suitcase. Fold each hanger area in, alternating bags so that each bag pads another bag's folded area.

5. Fill in corner spaces with scarves, stockings, and underwear.

Keep in mind the size of your suitcase. Too much empty space will allow your garments to shift within the suitcase, and too little room means crushed clothes. Both styles of packing will create wrinkling.

Upon arrival, immediately unpack clothing to keep it looking fresh and allow wrinkles to hang out. With your ensembles and separates already on hangers, unpacking will be a snap.

If you have time, hang especially wrinkled garments in the bathroom (away from the shower spray), turn on a hot shower and close the door. Wrinkles will probably disappear during a 15- to 20-minute steam bath. If they don't, use an iron for a few quick touch-ups.

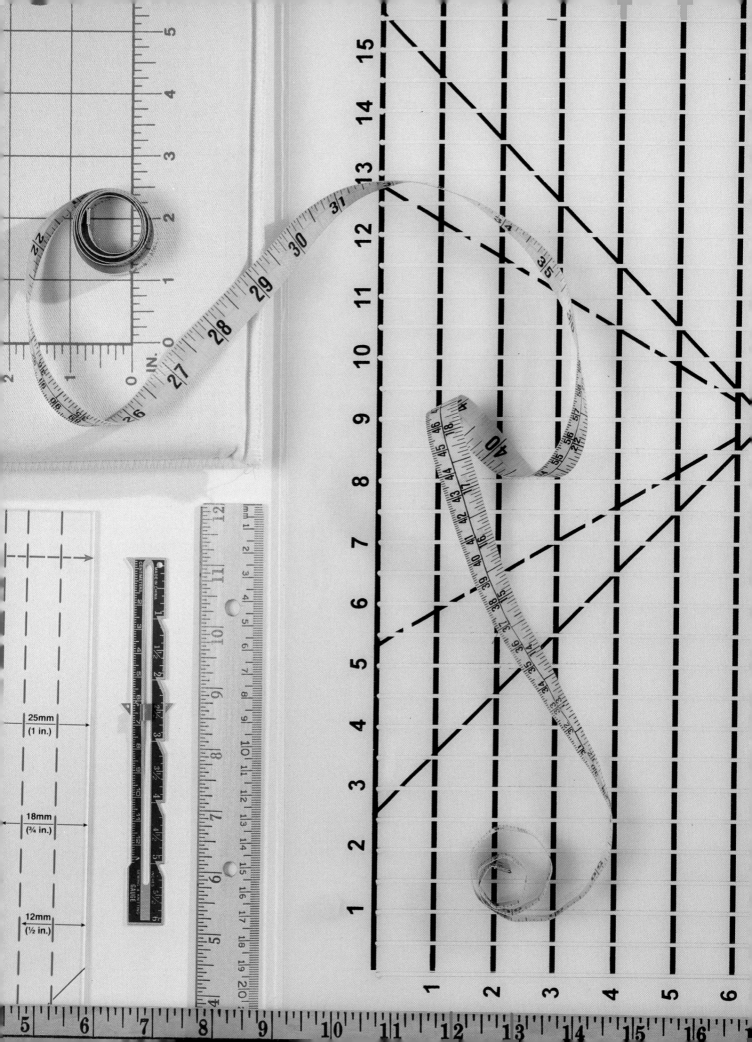

APPENDIX

Having information right at your fingertips

is always a timesaver. Photocopy the following lists

and charts to carry with you or tack on your bulletin board

for handy reference.

The long and short of it

Knowing what stitch length to use where is key to sewing successfully. However, this easy machine adjustment can sometimes be confusing because stitch length is measured two ways. Some machines measure in stitches per inch while others measure the length of the stitch.

When length is measured in stitches per inch, the range is usually from 6 to 20, plus "fine." The higher the number, the shorter the stitch. When length is measured by the length of the stitch, the range is usually from 0 to 4, 5, or 6. These numbers represent the length of each stitch in millimeters; the higher the number, the longer the stitch.

To choose the proper stitch length, consider fabric type and sewing technique. The normal stitch length for general-purpose sewing, including seams, is 10 to 12 stitches per inch or 2mm to 2.5mm. For stitch lengths used in other types of sewing, refer to the accompanying chart.

Stitch Equivalents and Uses

Stitch Length (mm)	Stitches per Inch	Uses
0	0	Stitching in place
.25	100	Satin stitching
.5	50	
1	25	
1.25	20	Reinforcement stitching
1.5	16	
2	12	General-purpose stitching
2.5	10	
3	8	Topstitching, easestitching, gathering
4	6	
5	5	
6	4	Basting

In addition:

• Use a longer stitch for heavyweight, dense, or tightly woven fabrics or when sewing leather, vinyl, or plastic, to avoid ripping along the seamline.

• Use a shorter stitch for lightweight fabrics and lace, curved seams, or seams on the bias.

Sheet smart

Need a wide seamless length of fabric for home decorating, costuming, or a special occasion? Try using sheets. Listed below are common sheet sizes and their dimensions:

Sheet Size	Flat Sheet Dimension
Crib	38"x52"
Cot	63"x96"
Twin	66"x96"
Full	81"x96"
Queen	90"x102"
King	108"x102"

Metric memory

Puzzled when trying to locate ⅝" on your needle-plate seam guide, where all the markings are in millimeters? Baffled by instructions telling you to sew a 6mm-wide serger stitch? Perplexed by the task of converting metric measurements? Refresh your memory with some sewing-related metric facts.

Fraction/Decimal/Metric Conversion

¹⁄₁₆"	=	.063"	=	1.5mm		
⅛"	=	.125"	=	3mm		
¼"	=	.25"	=	6mm		
⅜"	=	.375"	=	9mm		
½"	=	.5"	=	13mm		
⅝"	=	.625"	=	15mm		
¾"	=	.75"	=	19mm		
⅞"	=	.875"	=	21mm		
1"	=	1.0"	=	25mm		

To convert a figure not shown, multiply the decimal equivalent of the fraction by .25 to arrive at its millimeter equivalent; to determine the centimeter equivalent, multiply by 2.5.

Note: These conversions are rounded to the nearest millimeter—there are 25.4mm to 1".

Fabric foibles

Wondering what to do when the fabric you want isn't the same width as that suggested on the project pattern? This handy chart will help you decide how much fabric of a given width you will need to buy.

✉ **Note:** These figures represent an approximate conversion. For nap fabrics and one-way designs, add at least ¼ yard more. Pattern alterations, large fabric designs, large pattern pieces, and matching allowances are not factored in this chart.

Fabric Conversion

Fabric Width	35"–36"	39"	41"	44"–45"	50"	52"–54"	58"–60"
Number of yards needed	1¾	1½	1½	1⅜	1¼	1⅛	1
	2	1¾	1¾	1⅝	1½	1⅜	1¼
	2¼	2	2	1¾	1⅝	1½	1⅜
	2½	2¼	2¼	2⅛	1¾	1¾	1⅝
	2⅞	2½	2½	2¼	2	1⅞	1¾
	3⅛	2¾	2¾	2½	2¼	2	1⅞
	3⅜	3	2⅞	2¾	2⅜	2¼	2
	3¾	3¼	3⅛	2⅞	2⅝	2⅜	2¼
	4¼	3½	3⅜	3	2¾	2⅝	2⅜
	4½	3¾	3⅝	3⅛	3	2¾	2⅝
	4¾	4	3⅞	3⅝	3¼	2⅞	2¾
	5	4¼	4⅛	3⅞	3⅜	3⅛	2⅞

Inching along

If you become confused when trying to convert fractions of a yard to inches, pull out a copy of this chart at the fabric store and show the salesclerk you know your stuff!

Fraction of a Yard	Inches
1/16	2¼"
⅛	4½"
¼	9"
⅓	12"
⅜	13½"
½	18"
⅝	22½"
⅔	24"
¾	27"
⅞	31½"
1	36"

Ease, please

The measurements given on garment pattern envelopes offer little clue to the actual amount of ease you can anticipate having in a given silhouette. The chart below tells how much "extra" fabric you can expect over and above the actual body measurements given on the pattern envelope.

Ease Allowances

Description	Dresses/tops (bust)	Jackets (bust)	Coats (bust)	Garment (hip)
Close-fitting	0"–2⅞"	0"		1⅞"
Fitted	3"–4"	3¾"–4¼"	5¼"–6¾"	2"–3"
Semi-fitted	4⅛"–5"	4⅜"–5¾"	6⅞"–8"	3⅛"–4"
Loose fitting	5⅛"–8"	5⅞"–10"	8⅛"–12"	4⅛"–6"
Very loose fitting	more than 8"	more than 10"	more than 12"	more than 6"

Stop the strain

To prevent back and neck strain, make sure your work areas and equipment are at the correct height.

Correct Heights

Equipment	Correct Work Height		Minimum Work Area
	Adult*	Child (age 12)*	
Sewing machine bed	28"	25"	9" to right of right leg (at foot control) 9" to left of left leg
Chair	16"	13"	
Ironing board (for use while seated)	24"		
Cutting table	36"	32"	30"x36" (36"x72" is ideal)
Mirror	6' (distance from top to floor)		18"x60"

*Average height for adult: 5'5"; for 12-year-old child, 4'10½"

INDEX

SOURCE LIST

If the products mentioned in *Sew News Timesaving Tips* are not available in your local area, contact the companies below for mail-order information or to find the retailer nearest you.

Button-Ons™
PeM Corporation
11142 Thompson Ave.
Lenexa, KS 66219
(913) 599-6299

Buttons
Buttons and Things
24 Main St., Route 1
Freeport, ME 04032
(207) 865-4480

Diamond Eye Needle™
Nancy's Notions
PO Box 683
Beaver Dam, WI 53916-0683
(800) 833-0690

Even Cut™
J. A. Enterprises
322 Vindale Dr.
Dayton, OH 45440
(513) 426-2648

Fusible Roll Line Tape
Unique Techniques
3840 136th Ave., NE
Bellevue, WA 98005
(800) 557-5563

Heat-Away™ Brush Off Stabilizer
Sulky of America
3113 Broadpoint Dr.
Harbor Heights, FL 33983
(813) 629-3199

Heirloom Stitcher's Shape 'N Press™ Board
June Tailor
PO Box 208
Richfield, WI 53076-0208
(800) 844-5400

Hot Tape™
Distlefink Designs, Inc.
PO Box 24
South Britain, CT 06487
(203) 264-6384

Interior Expressions Iron-on Drapery Tapes by Dritz
Prym-Dritz Corp.
PO Box 5028
Spartanburg, SC 29204

Mönster Papper
The Sewing Place
PO Box 111446
Campbell, CA 95011
(800) 587-3937

Multiple Cording Guide
MarGale Sewing Specialties
5 Paradies Lane
New Paltz, NY 12561-4017
(914) 255-8020

Nifty Notions Appliqué Pins
Quilter's Resource, Inc.
PO Box 148850
Chicago, IL 60614
(312) 278-5695

Perfect Sew™
Palmer/Pletsch Associates
PO Box 12046
Portland, OR 97212
(503) 274-0687

Quilt-Safe Curved Basting Pins
Nancy's Notions
PO Box 683
Beaver Dam, WI 53916-0683
(800) 833-0690

Rotary Cutting Guide
Clotilde
2 Sew Smart Way, B-8031
Stevens Point, WI 54481-8031
(800) 772-2891

SlipNots™
Sew Unique
3045 S. 150th St.
Seattle, WA 98188
(206) 244-7934

Straight-Tape™
Nancy's Notions
PO Box 683
Beaver Dam, WI 53916-0683
(800) 833-0690

Strips Ahoy™ 100
Coming Attractions
3104 E. Camelback Rd. #213
Phoenix, AZ 85016
(602) 468-1938

Threads
Coats and Clark
30 Patewood Dr., Suite 351
Greenville, SC 29615
(803) 234-0331

Zippers
Coats and Clark
30 Patewood Dr., Suite 352
Greenville, SC 29615
(803) 234-0331